长岛民俗文化双语阅读

陈艳君　王红燕　付娟　编著

吉林大学出版社

·长春·

图书在版编目（CIP）数据

长岛民俗文化双语阅读：汉英对照 / 陈艳君，王红燕，付娟编著. -- 长春：吉林大学出版社，2021.9
ISBN 978-7-5692-8973-2

Ⅰ.①长… Ⅱ.①陈… ②王… ③付… Ⅲ.①英语－汉语－对照读物②风俗习惯－介绍－长岛县 Ⅳ.① H319.4：K

中国版本图书馆 CIP 数据核字（2021）第 209197 号

书　　　名：长岛民俗文化双语阅读

CHANGDAO MINSU WENHUA SHUANGYU YUEDU

作　　　者：陈艳君　王红燕　付　娟　编著
策划编辑：朱　进
责任编辑：张宏亮
责任校对：蔡玉奎
装帧设计：姜晓波
出版发行：吉林大学出版社
社　　　址：长春市人民大街 4059 号
邮政编码：130021
发行电话：0431-89580028/29/21
网　　　址：http://www.jlup.com.cn
电子邮箱：jdcbs@jlu.edu.cn
印　　　刷：北京兴星伟业印刷有限公司
开　　　本：787mm×1092mm　　1/16
印　　　张：10
字　　　数：160 千字
版　　　次：2021 年 9 月第 1 版
印　　　次：2021 年 9 月第 1 次
书　　　号：ISBN 978-7-5692-8973-2
定　　　价：48.00 元

目 录

第一单元　渔家习俗

Unit One　Fishing Customs

长岛的世代渔民,依靠全船人的共同劳作,闯海打鱼;凭借集体的智慧和力量,战风斗浪。几经出生入死,也屡屡化险为夷。特殊的生产和生活方式,养成粗犷、豪放、无私、质朴地闯海人的性格,也形成了特有的渔家习俗。

In Long Island, generations of fishermen, relying on the joint work of all the people on the boat,

图 1-1-1　上网出海

rushed into the sea to fish. They fought against the wind and the waves with their collective wisdom and strength. They always risked their lives, and repeatedly turned danger to safety. The special production made and lifestyle had cultivated the character of a rough, unrestrained, selfless and simple sea striver, and also formed a unique fisherman's customs.

第一课　上网出海
Lesson One　Going to the Sea with net

20世纪60年代以前,长岛县的渔业生产主要使用大风船,打风网,围捕鱼群。每年清明前后,渔民要出海去"东地"(黄海)打黄花鱼。一般要提前几天上网(把渔网装上船)。

Before the 1960s, the fishery production in Changdao County were mainly achieved by using large sailboats and wind nets for fishing. Every year around Qingming festival, fishermen go to the "East Land" (Yellow Sea) to catch yellow croaker. It is generally necessary to set up the net a few days in advance (to bring the fishnet onto the ship).

图 1-1-2　扬帆起航

几百竿子的大网,分扎成十多捆,分堆在海滩(或广场)上。事先用草(谷秸)扎成一把,再准备一只葫芦瓢,内盛荞麦面。准备就绪,便敲锣,鸣放鞭炮。

A large net made of several hundreds of poles was divided into more than ten bundles, and piled on the beach (or square). A handful of tied straw (grain straw) was prepared in advance, and then a gourd scoop is prepared with soba noodles loaded in it, after which you hit the gong and set off firecrackers.

一人擎起点着的杆草火把,围着网堆跑,另一人跟在后面,手持面瓢边跑边撒荞麦面,围跑一圈后,二人跑到船上,在"赶膛"上转一圈,撒面人紧赶几步,把瓢扣到持火把人的头上,全体上网人放声大笑,高喊着:"扣着了""打满了"。表示下网打着鱼群了。点燃杆草有驱邪消灾之意。接着"号头"领叫起"上网"的渔号,全体船员应和着渔号,肩扛渔网,手擎捞鱼兜子,依次上船,待渔网全部装上船后,再燃放鞭炮,船员都拿起捞鱼兜子,从网里作捞鱼倒向船舱的动作。标志着网满装船,喜获丰收。

One person held the starting torch and ran around the net pile, while the other followed, holding the noodle scoop while sprinkling the soba noodles; the two ran on the boat after a round, and then turned on the "Gantang" a circle; the man who sprinkled flour hurried up for a few steps and made the scoop upside down on the torch holder's head. All the people laughed loudly and shouted: "It's finished." and "It's full." It means that you have caught a school of fish with the net. Kindling the straw has the meaning of exorcising evil and eliminating disasters. Then the "leader" called up the fishing horn for "seting up the net". All the crew members responded with the fishing horn, carried the nets on their shoulders, grabbed the fish pockets with their hands, and boarded the boat in turn. After the nets are all loaded on the boat, the firecrackers will be set off. They all picked up the fishing pockets and acted as if they have caught fishes and made them pouerd into the cabin. It signifies that the net is full and a good harvest is realized.

上网的大船,大小桅杆上挂起大小红吊子(长幅红布),船体各处贴"红对子"和大、小"福"字。上网时,整个海口渔港,红旗招展,锣鼓喧天,鞭炮齐鸣,渔号声,喊叫声,谈笑声,连成一片,场面十分壮观。

The big and small real slings (the long red cloth) was hung on their masts on large boats with net. And "red couplet" and large and small "Fu" characters were posted everywhere on the hull. When equipping the net, the entire fishing port was full of red flags, gongs and drums, firecrackers, fishing horns, shouts and chattering, forming a speclacular scene.

出海时,挂起大小红吊子,燃放鞭炮,扬帆起航,摇大撸的叫起摇橹的渔号。先去妈祖庙上香拜庙,祈求海神娘娘保佑出门发财,四季平安。再到"南帮"(烟台、蓬莱等地)港口上"吃米"(上足给养)。多数船只则买猪杀肉,一为祈祝高产丰收,二为改善船员生活,强壮身体。根据船员人数,将猪心割成数份,每人一块分食,谓之"团结一心"。

When going out to sea, we hung up big and small red slings, set off firecrackers, set sail, and shook the fishing horn. Firstly, they went to the Matsu Temple to worship the incense temple, and pray for the Sea God Empress to bless them make a fortune and safety, then we went to the "Nanbang" (Yantai, Penglai, etc.) ports to "chimi" (make enough supplement). Most fishers bought pig for meat, for wishing a high-yield harvest, and improving the life of the crew and making their bodies more stronger. According to the number of crew members, the pig's heart was cut into several portions, and each person shared a piece of food, which is called "united as one".

图 1-1-3 祈求发财

出海下的第一网捕到鱼后,挑四条大的放到油锅里烙后蒸熟,装盘摆放在船头,烧香纸,放鞭炮,全体船员换好衣服跪拜船头,将鱼投倒海中,敬献给海神龙王,祈求四季发财。

After catching the fish with the first casting, we selected four large ones and put them in a frying pan and made them steamed, which then would be put on the front of boat, making the incense paper burned and the firecrackers set off. All the crew changed their clothes, bowed down to the bow and casting the fish into the sea to offer it respectfully to the Dragon King of the Sea God, praying for wealth in the four seasons.

思考与实践

观看长岛民俗表演,描写一篇渔民上网出海的文章。

Thinking and practice

Please watch the folklore performance on Changdao and make an article about sea fishing.

第二课　发财归来

Lesson 2　Coming back with fortune

　　海上生产个月有余,期间,或一网两船,或几网满载,活打鲜卖。鱼群向西地洄游,一季"货海"结束,除去费用开销,算得高产丰收的,便是"出门发财"了。于是,在外地港口,置办货物。抓猪买菜,打酒购粮。开饷给船员购买物品。一切齐备,便起锚返航。桅杆上挂起暗示发财的大红吊子,唱着《发财》的渔号,喜气洋洋地返程回家。岛上的人远远望着挂着大吊子的渔船,根据船形特征,就知道某船发财回来了。如果是挂起双吊子,昭示特大丰收——发大财了。不一会儿,喜讯便会传遍全岛各村。这时候,港口里,迎船的,接人的,搬货的,报喜的,人流如潮,欢声笑语充满港湾渔家。

图 1-2-1　发财归来

　　The production at sea lasts one month or more. During the period, one net for two ships, or a few nets are fully loaded, and they are sold fresh. Schools of fish are migrating to the west, at the end of the "sea of goods" season, deducting expenses, the high yield and good harvest represent a fortune. So, purchasing goods in foreign ports, grabbing pigs, buying food and wine, paying and buying items for the crew. Everything is ready, then anchor and return. The big red sling was hung on the mast, as a hint for getting rich, singing the fishing horn of "Getting Fortune", and returning home joyfully. The people on the island looked at the fishing boat with slings from a far knew that a certain boat had made a fortune based on the features and shapes of boats. If it is a pair of slings, it indicates a huge harvest —— a fortune. In a short while, the good news will spread to all villages on the island. At this time, in the harbour, the people who greeted the boat, received people, moved the goods, and announced the news, were like a tide, and the laughter filled up the whole harbor and families of fishermen.

太阳升起,港湾一片通红。龙王庙（一般都建在港湾滩头）前热闹非凡。大旗杆上升起龙王旗,锣鼓喧天,鞭炮齐鸣,香火缭绕。龙王塑像前的供桌上,摆上了祭祀供品。发财的船主带领全体船员,上香跪拜以后。一旁的屠床上,按上了活猪,杀发财猪,祭祀海神,感谢龙王的恩赐,祈求更大丰收。

The sun rose and the harbor was all red. A bustling scene shows in front of the Dragon King Temple (usually built on the beachhead of the harbor). The dragon king flag was raised on the big flagpole, gongs and drums were noisy, firecrackers rang, and incense filled the sky. Sacrificial offerings were placed on the altar table in front of the dragon king statue. The rich shipowner led all the crew to bow for praying. On the slaughtering bed, live pigs were pressed for killing, to sacrifice the god of the sea as gratitude for the dragon king's gift, and praying for a greater harvest.

祭神仪式刚毕,龙王庙前支起几只大锅,便粗柴旺火地烧将起来。猪肉、粉条、青菜烧成大菜,小米干饭也做若干。猪头送到船老大（船长）家里,猪蹄分给二把头（副船长）。一腔"下水"和部分猪肉做成各样大盘精菜,邀请村里有名望人士、"坐坞"（退休）的老船长,以及本船船员,分坐数桌,大吃海喝起来。全村的儿童,自带碗筷,列队领饭盛菜。村里的困难户和过路行人等均可分领。在过去那些年代里,能这样白吃一顿小米干饭,猪肉炖粉条子,可算是上佳的美餐了。儿童们特别爱赶热

图 1-2-2　岸上分拣

闹,捧着大碗,装满黄黄的米饭,白生生的粉条,绿绿的青菜,红白相间大块猪肉,有滋有味地吃着,欢笑着,跑着,叫着……

As soon as the ceremony was completed, a few cauldrons were erected in front of the Dragon King Temple and the wood was burnt vigorously. Pork, vermicelli and green vegetables were cooked into main dishes, and rice was also cooked. The pig's head was sent to the the ship's boss (captain), and the pig's trotter was sent to the vice captain. The pluck and part of the pork are made into various dishes, and the famous people in the village, the retired captain and the crew of the ship were invited to sit at several tables, eat and drink. The children in the village brought their own tableware and chopsticks to get meals and serve dishes. The households in poverty and pedestrians in the village can be served. In those past years, it was a great meal to be able to eat rice and pork and vermicelli like this. Children especially liked to rush to the fun, holding big bowls, filled with yellow rice, white raw vermicelli, green vegetables, chunks of pork, eating with a sense of taste, laughing, running, and screaming ...

海沿边,流淌着油腻,空气中,飘散着肉香。这真是,一船发财,全村人都分享着丰收的喜悦。

The seaside was greasy, and the smelling of meat wafts in the air. It was true that the whole village was sharing the joy of a bumper harvest when a boat makes fortune.

思考与实践

Thinking and practice

渔民发财归来有什么特点?

What are the characteristics of fishermen returning from a fortune?

根据课文内容展开自己的想象,描写一篇渔民发财归来的景象。

Develop your own imagination based on the content of the text, and describe a scene of fishermen returning from making fortune.

第三课　海上礼让
Lesson 3　Comity on the sea

　　长岛人出门便要乘船渡海，在海上行船，特别讲究礼让。两船在海上相遇，都有一套礼让的规矩。两船对驶，总是大船让小船，顺风船让逆风船。晚上行船或抛锚停泊，总要点亮船上的桅灯，谨防船只相撞受损。渔船下网，航行的船应

绕开网地。风围网大海市，渔场上，千帆竞发，百船穿梭，渔船的大桅顶上，立有"鱼眼"（登高探视鱼群），船舱里有人耳贴船底（寻听鱼群的叫声），搜索"鱼信"，寻找大鱼群，随时准备下网围扑。有时候，一个大鱼群，被两只或几只渔船，同时探到，或略先稍后发现，只要有船已先下网，其他船自觉让出网区，决

图1-3　海上礼让

不"掏网心"，截鱼群。另选相邻的海域下网围扑。尽管错过了最好时机，或者偏离鱼群中心，影响产量，但绝不破坏规矩，无礼争抢。有的船，围住了特大鱼群，自己"捞起了"（满载），立即拉"招旗"，招呼邻近船前来捞鱼，不管相识与否，也无须感激酬谢。多者一网数船，大家喜气洋洋，船船满载归港。

People on Changdao county had to take a boat to cross the sea when they went out and they are especially courteous on the sea. When two ships met at sea, there was always a set of comity rules. When two boats went in opposite directions, the big boat gave way to the small one, and the downwind boat to the upwind one. When sailing at night or anchoring, the masthead lights on the ship would be always lighted up to prevent collisions and damage. When the fishing net was thrown off the boat, other sailing boats should bypass the net. The wind seines the sea and the fishing grounds. Thousands of sails were flying and hundreds of boats were shuttled. On the top of the big mast of the fishing boat, there were "fish eyes" (climbing to see the fish), and there were people in the cabin putting the ear onto the bottom of boat (listening the calling of fishes), searching for "fish letter", looking for fishing for large fish schools, and being ready to lay down the net for fishing. Sometimes, a large school of fish was spotted by two or several fishing boats at the same time, or discovered a little later; as long as one of the boats had already got off the net first, other boats voluntarily left the net area, and never "pulled out the net core" or make the school of fish intercepted. Instead, they would choose another adjacent sea area for fishing was deviated. Although the best time was missed, or the center of the fish school, making the production affected, but the rules would never be broken and rudely scrambling would never occur. Some boats surrounded the huge school of fish, fully loaded, and immediately raised the "flag" to greet the neighboring boats for fishing here. No matter whether they knew each other or not, there was no need to be grateful or rewarded. Sometimes, one net of fish catched can be shared by several boats, everyone was happy, and the boats returned with full loads.

　　搭乘便船,也是长岛人的一种特殊风俗。岛上群众过渡或远行,除了固定的职业性客船、渡船外,顺路的渔船,运输船等都让人随便搭乘过海(叫坐便船),捎运货物。这种坐"便船"的乘客,不但不用付船费,在路远的航行途中,船上还免费供给饮食。如是渔船捕鱼归来,还专门多做些新鲜海货,让搭乘者品尝白吃。晕船者,会得到船员的照顾,老、幼、病、弱者,常被安排在船员的睡铺上休息。一觉醒来,已到达目的地,倍感船家渔民的慷慨与无私。

Taking a free boat is also a special custom of Changdao Islanders. When the people on the island transit or travel far, in addition to the fixed professional passenger ships and ferry boats, the fishing boats and transport ships that go along the way would all take people over the sea freely (called free boats) and carry goods for them. This kind of "handy boat" passengers, don't have to pay the boat fare, besides they also can be offered free food and drink on board during the long voyage. If the fishing boat returns from fishing, more fresh seafood would be prepared, for free tasting of passengers. Seasick people will be taken care of by the crew, and the old, young, sick, and weak were often arranged to rest in the crew's sleeping bunk. When woke up, the destination was already reached, increasing their feeling in generosity and selflessness of the boatmen and fishermen.

思考与实践

Thinking and practice

通过阅读长岛民俗海上礼让你有何感想，谈谈你的感受。

Talk about your feelings by reading the Changdao Island Folklore Comity on the sea.

第四课　海上救助
Lesson Four　Rescue in the sea

　　在闯海打鱼的生涯中，经常遭遇风浪灾害。渔民们需要全船团结一心，奋力抗灾自救，也需要别船他人的救助。长期以来，普遍形成了海上自觉救助的习俗。

　　In the career of fishing in the sea, people often encountered wind and wave disasters. The fishermen in the whole ship are required to unite as one, struggle to fight the

图 1-4-1　海上救助

disaster and save themselves, and of course they also need the rescue from others. For a long time, the custom of conscious rescue at sea has generally formed.

　　在大海上，一旦发现遇难的渔船，即使素不相识，也会毫不犹豫拼死相救。1973 年 2 月，砣矶岛井口村"长渔七号"船，抗着 10 级暴风雪，顶着寒流冰冻，舍生忘死地抢救了 4 只辽宁省长海县的小渔船，将 16 名遇难的外省渔民全部救起，受到山东省委和军区的表彰。

　　On the sea, once you find a fishing boat in distress, even if you don't know each other, you will not hesitate to fight desperately for rescue. In February 1973, the "Changyu No. 7" boat in Jingkou Village, Tuoji Island, resisting a 10th grade blizzard and being confronted with cold snap and frosts, sacrificed itself to rescue 4 small fishing boats in Changhai County, Liaoning Province, and saved 16 fishermen in danger from other provinces. It was commended by Shandong

Provincial Party Committee and the Military Command.

长岛人民,舍己为人,无私无畏,不断地谱写着海上救助的新篇章。2003年2月22日14时30分,大连渤海船务公司所属"辽旅渡7"客货滚装船,从

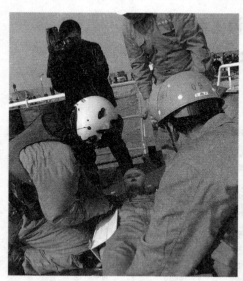

旅顺开往龙口途中,在长岛县砣矶岛西北约10海里处,遭风浪翻船遇险。长岛县委、县政府立即成立抢险领导小组,在县领导的指挥下,展开了一场惊心动魄的海上大营救。砣矶镇党委书记王成强,带领6条渔船,劈风斩浪,以最快速度赶到出事海域。他们顶着狂风恶浪,冒着生命危险,采用放缆绳,抛救生圈等办法,搭救遇难者。有的渔民不顾自身安危,腰拴绳索,爬下船舷,探身伸手从寒涛浊浪中抱起一个个落水人员。驻军某部8002艇,也奉命赶到现场,艇上全体官兵和7名大钦岛的志愿者,也加入风浪中救人

图 1-1-2　扬帆起航

的战斗行列。经过5个多小时生与死的搏斗,在遇难船只沉没的情况下,81名遇难者全部获救。创造了海难救助史上的又一个奇迹。

The people of Chang Island are selfless and fearless, continue to write new chapters in maritime rescue. At 14:30 on February 22, 2003, the mixed passenger and cargo ship "Liaolvdu 7" subordinate to Dalian Bohai Shipping Company was on the way from Lvshun to Longkou. At about 10 nautical miles northwest of Tuoji Island in Changdao County, it was hit by wind and waves. and capsized in distress. The Changdao County Party Committee and government immediately set up a rescue leading group, and under the command of the county leaders, a thrilling rescue at sea was launched. Wang Chengqiang, secretary of the Party Committee of Tuoji Town, led six fishing boats through the wind and waves, and rushed to the sea area where the accident occurred as quickly as possible. They braved the violent winds and waves, risked their lives, and used methods such as laying cables and throwing life buoys to rescue the victims. Regardless of their own safety, some fishermen tied ropes at their waists, climbed off the ship's side, leaned forward and reached out to pick up the people who fell into the water from the cold and turbid waves. No. 8002 boat from certain portion of the garrison was also ordered to rush to the scene. All officers and soldiers on the boat and 7 volunteers from Daqin Island also joined the battle to save people in the storm. After more than five hours of life-and-death struggle, all 81 victims were rescued from the ship sank, creating another miracle in the history of shipwreck rescue.

海上忘我无私的救助,是长岛人的传统美德。六十年代以前,渔民有下伏钩、下秋钩钓鱼的生产作业。一只大风船,一般装带四只小船(俗称"子船",载重2吨左右,3、4人作业),来到远洋深水渔场,大船选一中心地站锚,小船到周围海域单独下拦钩生产。有时,风浪突起,小船来不及赶回,大船便张蓬加橹,四处寻找。这种时候,不管遇到谁家的小船,都主动赶向前去,将其拖带,救人上船,视为自己的船员,悉心照顾。有时,为追赶被风浪卷走的别家小船,远离自己的作业区域,耽误了宝贵的时间,增加了找回自己小船的难度。

Selfless rescue at sea is a traditional virtue of Long Islanders. Before the 1960s, fishermen used to carry out production operations for fishing in dog days and autumn, A big sailboat usually carried four small boats (commonly known as "sub-ships", with a load of about 2 tons, and operated by 3 or 4 people) to deep-water ocean fishing ground. The big boat chose a central station to anchor, and the boat put the hooks in the surrounding waters. Sometimes, when the wind and waves blew up, the small boats were too late to rush back, and the big boat would spread out and look around. At this time, no matter any small boat encountered, they would take the initiative to rush forward, tow it, save people aboard, treated it as its own crew member, and take care of it. Sometimes, in order to catch up with other boats that were swept away by the wind and waves, they always stay away from their own work area, which delayed precious time and increased the difficulty in retrieving their own boat.

在海上,发现罹难的尸体,不论是否完整,他们都能停产处理。船员们拿出干净的铺盖、衣物,将尸体收殓起来,送上岸,或找失事船只,送交其亲属,或选地掩埋,入土为安。

At sea, if the dead bodies were found, regardless of whether they were intact or not, they can stop their own production for processing of corpse. The crew took out clean bedding and clothing, collected the corpse and sent it ashore, or looked for the wrecked ship, sent it to their relatives, or chose a place to bury it, and put it in the soil in peace.

鱼汛期间,常有小船流走,网具丢失的情况发生。别的渔船在海上发现,或看船号,查标记,或算潮流,观风向,估计失物从何方漂流而来,千方百计地寻找失主,完璧归赵。有时,宁肯耽误一刻千金的捕鱼时间,决不让失主错过汛期。有一种放流网作业,大都在傍晚下网,鱼虾晚上起水,便于网鱼扎虾。渔船扯住网绠,带着上千米长的网片,在夜海中漂流。偶遇风扯浪打,或是客、商船只通过,拉断了的渔网,便随流漂走,一夜之间,便无踪影。天亮收网时,别的船拾到了,会把这断网里的鱼虾,单独摘取装舱,待找到失主,一并奉还。

During the fishing season, small boats often drifted away and nets were lost frequently. When other fishing boats were found them on the sea, the ship's number found, mark checked, or the tide calculated, the wind direction watched can be based to estimate where the lost property drifted from, and did everything possible to find the owner and returned them back. Sometimes, they would rather delay a moment of fishing time, and never let the owner miss the flood season. There was a discharge net operation, where most of the nets were cast in the evening, for convenience of netting of fish and shrinp, which used to swim up the winter then. The fishing boat grabbed the net stem and drifted in the night with a thousand-meter-long net piece. In the event of wind and waves encountered, or the passing of passenger or merchant ships, causing fishing net broken, then the fish would drift away, and there would be no trace overnight. When it's time to pick up the net at dawn, if other boats picked up the fish and shrimp in the broken net separately, they would put them back together. When the owner was found, they would be returned together.

思考与实践

Thinking and practice

2003 年 2 月 22 日，在长岛海域发生了一起严重的海难事故，长岛人民火速营救，81 名人员全部获救，创造了海难救助史上又一奇迹，史称"2·22"海难大营救。搜集这方面资料，完整记叙这次营救过程。

On February 22, 2003, a serious shipwreck occurred in the waters of Changdao. All 81 people were rescued by the people of Changdao quickly, creating another miracle in the history of shipwreck rescue. The history is called "2.22" shipwreck rescue. Collect this information and fully record and narrate the rescue process.

第五课 渔家忌讳
Lesson 5 Fishermen's Taboos

过去,在落后的生产力、难以抗拒的自然灾害面前,渔家特别迷信,也有许多忌讳。渔民的生产和生活上的言行十分谨慎,多说"彩头话",禁忌不吉利的

语言。忌说"翻"和"扣",意在怕船在海里翻扣过来。要表达它们的意思则说"划"字,常用"划身""划过来"。渔船上的帆,因与"翻"同音,所以也不叫"帆",而称为"蓬"。渔船卸完鱼,不能说"卸完了""没有了",而要说"满了"。捕鱼时,鱼网全部撒到海里后,不能说"网下完了",而要说"丈杆子(风网头上的木叉子)

图1-5 渔家忌讳

朝前喽,一网两船了"或者说"满了""这网起了"。在海上见到鲸鱼,不能直呼其名,用手指点,而应尊称为"老兆""老人家"或"财神爷爷",即使鲸鱼碰到网上或在船边游窜,也不能出口不逊或稍有伤害。而要做祷告,祈求财神爷保佑丰收发财。敲锣放鞭炮,往海里撒米面,敬送它离开。因为,鲸鱼为了寻猎食物,常跟踪鱼群,渔民可根据它的活动范围找到鱼群,所以把它奉为不可冒犯的神物。

In the past, in the face of backward productivity and irresistible natural disasters, fishermen were especially superstitious and had many taboos. The fishermen were very cautious in their words and deeds during their production and life, saying more "colorful speech" and abstaining from inauspicious words. Avoid saying "turn over" and "reverse", for fear that the ship will overturn in the sea. To express their meaning, the word "draw" was used, and "draw one's body" and "draw over" were often used. The sails on fishing boats were not called "fan" because they are homophonous with "turning over", so called "peng" instead. After the fishing boat had finished unloading of fish, one cannot say "completed unloading" or "no more", but "full". When fishing, after all the nets were thrown into the sea, you can't say "the net is over", but say "the pole (the wooden fork on the head of the wind net) was facing forward, and one net in two boats" or "full" "This net is up". When you saw a whale in the sea, you can't just call its name and used your fingers to point it. Instead, you should call it "Old Zhao", "Old Man" or "Grandpa God of Wealth". Even if the whale hit the net or swam on the side of a boat, you can't say anything bad or make it slightly hurt. And to pray, pray for the God of Wealth to bless the abundance and receive wealth. Knocking the gong and setting off firecrackers, or spreading rice and noodles into the sea, for making it swimming away. Because whales often followed schools of fish for hunting, fishermen can find schools of fish according to their range of moving, so they were regarded as an unoffendable fetish.

　　渔民在行船中,禁止唱情歌,吹口哨,不能将手背在身后,表现出一种心不在焉,思想松弛的举动。"背"和"顺"相悖。渔民出海,希望一帆风顺,时时事事顺心如愿。"背"意味着违背意愿,运气不佳,发财无望。背手还有"打背网"之说。在船上行走,脚步要轻,禁忌跑跳嬉闹。吃饭时,不能把筷子放在碗上。这和海难中,渔船免桅相似。(渔船遇到特大风浪,无力抗争时,只好放倒桅杆,倒拖铁锚,随风漂流,听天由命。俗称"下涝子")渔家的锅、碗、盆、勺不能扣放,意有翻船之兆。人不准坐在大柱子（船体竖立的木桩）和船头上,这有不敬之意和不祥之兆。平日里,忌讳老婆（妇女）跨船、跨渔网、渔具。因为老婆的"婆"字同"破"字同音。

Fishermen were not allowed to sing love songs, whistle, or put their hands behind them when they were on the boat moved to show a kind of absent-minded and lax thought. "Back" and "Smooth" were contrary. The fishermen went out to sea, hoped that everything would be smooth and current affairs would go as they wished. "Back" means going against the will, bad luck, and hopeless to make a fortune. There was also the saying of "playing the back net" by back hand. When walking on the boat, the steps should be light, and running and jumping should not be allowed. Do not put chopsticks on the bowl when eating. This was similar that in a shipwreck, the fishing boat was free of mast. (When the fishing boat encountered extreme wind and waves and was unable to fight, it had to lower its mast, dragged its anchor, drifted with the wind, and resigned. Commonly known as "Xialaozi") The fisherman's pots, bowls, basins, and spoons cannot be put upside down, which meant the boat was intentionally capsized. People were not allowed to sit on the big pillars (the wooden stakes erected on the hull of the ship) and the bow, which was disrespectful and ominous. On weekdays, it was taboo for wives (women) to cross boats, fish nets, and fishing gear. Because the prounciation of the Chinese character "wife" is the same with that of "break".

现在,许多忌讳已逐渐消失。

Now, many taboos have gradually disappeared.

思考与实践

Thinking and practice

列举海岛风俗中有哪些忌讳？

List the taboos in island customs.

第六课 渔家方言
Lesson 6 Dialect of Fisherman

长岛县是山东省唯一的海岛县。语言的地方变体,直接、间接的受当地地地理位置、自然条件、生产生活方式和文化教育、风俗习惯的影响。因此,方言具有浓郁的海洋气息和海岛特色。

Changdao County is the only island county in Shandong Province. Local variants of language are directly and indirectly affected by local geographic location, natural conditions, production mode and lifestyle, culture, education, and customs. Therefore, the dialect has strong oceanic and island characteristics.

图1-6 渔家方言

长岛地方方言直接地反映了当地风俗习惯。在日常生活中,语言禁忌十分明显。器皿里盛的东西用完了,叫"满出来了";碟碗等陶瓷、玻璃器具打碎了,叫"笑了";饺子煮破了,叫"挣了";打煤,叫"打砟子";倒水,叫"压水";把东西翻了个个儿,叫"划以戗";升帆,叫"掌篷";抛锚,叫"给锚"……可见"完了""破了""碎了""翻""帆""煤"等忌语,多采用回避法,改用反义词或彩头话来表达。充分表现了海岛人民图吉利、忌邪恶和向往太平、富有地愿望。在日常生活中形容词显得丰富、具体、贴切,具有较强地表现力。

The local dialect of Changdao directly reflects local customs and habits. In daily life, the language taboos are very obvious. When the contents in the utensils are used up, it can called "full out"; the breaking of dishes, bowls and other ceramics and glass utensils is called "laughing"; when the dumplings are boiled to be broken, it can be called "earned"; coal is called "ballast"; Pour water, called "pressing water"; turning things over, called "making it placed in opposite pasition"; raising a sail, called "operating the mat roofing"; dropping anchor, called "giving anchor"... Taboo words such as "ended", "broken", "smashed", "turned", "fan", and "coal" are often evasive, and should be replaced by antonyms or lucky words instead. It fully demonstrated the island people's desire for good luck, fear of evil, and yearning for peace and wealth. In daily life, adjectives used are rich, specific, appropriate and strongly expressive.

酸、甜、苦、辣、咸、鲜叫作：焦酸、西甜、烈苦、死辣、生咸、溜鲜；

香、臭、腥、涩、霉、臊叫作：喷香、生臭、虾腥、巴涩、衣霉、乔臊；

胖、瘦、粗、细、大、小叫作：大胖、精瘦、老粗、节细、老大、不点儿；

臭、俊、软、硬、稀、稠叫作：劣丑、葱俊、虚软、锭硬、流稀、挺厚；

红、黄、蓝、白、青、紫叫作：赤红、焦黄、妖蓝、条白、显青、血紫；

Sour, sweet, bitter, spicy, salty, and fresh are expressed by: pyro-sour, very sweet, extremely bitter, deadly spicy, raw salty, and purely fresh;

Fragrant, smelly, fishy, astringent, mildew, and odor of urine are called: delicious, unpleasantly smelly, prawn fishy, very astringent, moldy, and strong odor of urine;

Fat, thin, thick, thin, big, and small are called: big fat, lean, very thick, very thin, extiemely bog, a little bit;

Ugly, handsome, soft, hard, thin, and thick are called: very ugly, brilliant, virtual soft, hard, runny, and very thick;

Red, yellow, blue, white, blue, and purple are called: crimson, burnt yellow, demon blue, striped white, bright blue, blood purple;

海岛方言除语言、词汇特殊外，还表现为语言结构规律不同。同是表达一个意思，但结构不一。如，这东西"很高"，可说"极好儿高""成子高""好没高""老高矮""大老高""老鼻子高"等句式。有的词，表现程度不同。如平，溜平，溜平溜平；实，老实，老老实实，其表现程度具有递增、强调之别。有的词，用否定肯定法。如，细，叫"不粗细"；浅，叫"不深浅"。其表现程度具有递减，深化之能。

In addition to special language and vocabulary, the island dialects also show different patterns of language structure. Although express the same meaning, different structures are used. For example, if this thing is "high", There are several sentence patterns for you to describe the extent of height, such as extremely high, very high, etc. Some words express different degrees. Such as flat, smooth, very smooth; solid, honest, very honest, the degree of performance is increasing and emphasized. Some words use negative affirmation. For example, thin is called "not coarse"; shallow is called "not deep". Its performance can be decreased and deepened progressively.

思考与实践

Thinking and practice
结合实际谈谈长岛方言的特点。
Talk about the characteristics of Changdao dialect in light of reality.

第七课 渔家节日
Lesson 7　Fisherman's Festival

龙凤日正月二十五为龙凤日。传说此日龙翻身,农家禁做农活,妇女禁做针线活,以防伤龙骨。中午吃龙凤面或饺子,包子。渔村早晨吃年糕,并将蒜秸、红布钱传成串,挂在小孩帽上或身上,称"串牛尾"。渔民多以次日的风向卜测渔业的丰歉。

Dragon and Phoenix Day — The twenty-fifth of the first lunar month is Dragon and Phoenix Day. Legend had it that today the dragon turned over, farm work is forbidden, and women were prohibited to do needlework to prevent damage to the dragon's bone. Eating dragon and phoenix noodles or dumplings at moon. The people live in fishing village eat rice cakes in the morning, and made garlic straws and red cloth money skewered, and hung them on children's hats or bodies, called "skewers of oxtail". The fishermen mostly used the wind direction on the next day to predict the abundance of the fishery.

人七日——正月逢七为人七日,人们多以此日天气晴阴卜测当年身体的好坏。初七管儿童,十七管中年人,二十七个老年人。人七日中午吃煎糕和面条。

二月二——农历二月初二,俗称"龙抬头"。此日,男女均停止劳作,以防伤龙骨龙眼。清晨,各户用灶灰在院中或门口画粮食囤子,称"二月二,打画地","囤子"内放五谷杂粮,用石头或瓦片盖住,象征五谷满仓,早饭时,人们用面条和煎好的年糕供奉土地神。此日,可以吃春节做的"圣虫""圣饼"。媳妇要走娘家,男人要理发(称剃龙头)。

Seventh related days for people — The seven related days in the first lunar month are involved; people always predicted their health in that year according to the weather on this day (sunny or cloudy). The seventh day is targeted at children, the seventeenth day at middle-aged people, and the twenty-seventh day at old aged people. People ate fried cakes and noodles at noon on the seven related days.

Lunar February 2nd Festival — The second day of the second month of the lunar calendar, commonly known as "the dragon head raising day". On this day, both men and women stopped working to prevent damage to the dragon's bone and eyes. In the early morning, households used stove ash to draw grain stocks in the courtyard or at the door, which was called "February 2, drawing land". The stocks were filled with grains and covered with stones or tiles, symbolizing the full grain storage. At breakfast, people used noodles and fried rice cakes to worship the god of the earth. On this day, you can eat the "animal shaped cakes" prepared during the Spring Festival. The daughter-in-law had to go to her family's house, and the man had to have a haircut (called shaved dragon head).

入伏——每年初伏伊始，称"入伏"。此日，多吃面条，民间有"立秋的饺子，入伏的面"之谣。

图 1-7-1　拌面　　　　图 1-7-2　炸酱面　　　　图 1-7-3　过水面

Beginning of dog days — the first day in the hottest part of summer. On this day, to eat more noodles. There was a saying that "dumplings in the beginning of autumn, and noodles in the first day of dog days".

七月七农历七月初七，俗称过"七七"，亦称"乞巧节"。农村七月初七过节；渔村七月初六过节，初七媳妇回娘家。节日磕巧果，做巧芽汤，蒸巧饽饽，吃饺子。旧时，姑娘多在乞巧节前相聚，做"乞巧"准备，用纸剪制各种工艺品，组成"巧篷"。节日期间把巧篷挂于屋里，上有狮子、斗鸡、凤凰、

图 1-7-4　巧篷

鲤鱼跳龙门、戏出子、转灯、金钟灯,晚饭后,姑娘们着新衣聚于屋内,明灯蜡烛,唱乞巧歌做拉巧游艺,其间观者络绎不绝。夜深,姑娘们取井水分喝,用芝麻芽纫针放置水上漂花乞巧。此活动一般延续4天左右,有的海岛村外表演。拉巧活动50年代消失。

July 7 The seventh day of the seventh month of the lunar calendar is commonly known as "Qiqi", also known as "Qi Qiao Festival". Rural holidays were celebrated on the seventh day of July of the lunar calendar; in fishing villages, the festival would be celebrated on the sixth day of July, and the daughter-in-law return to her family on the seventh day, making various cakes by molds, sprout soup, steamed sweet pastry, and eating dumplingson the festival. In the old days, girls mostly gathered before the Qiqiao Festival to make preparations for "praying" and made various handicrafts by paper cutting to form "Qiao Canopies". During the festival, the Qiao Canopies were hung in the house, on which the followings are presented, including lions, cockfighting, phoenixes, carps jumping on the dragon gate, acting, turning lights, and admiralty lights. After dinner, the girls gathered in the house in their new clothes, lit candles, sang songs for praying, and pulled. There are endless crowds of viewers during the skillful entertainment. In the middle of the night, the girls took water from the well and used sesame buds to put flowers on the water to beg for cleverness. This activity generally last about 4 days, and some perform outside the island village. These activities disappeared in the 1950s.

思考与实践

Thinking and practice
想一想渔家还有哪些传统节日,说说其特点。
Think about the traditional festivals of fishermen and talk about their characteristics.

第二单元 民俗活动·风味小吃

Unit 2 Folklore Activities•Special Snacks

体会渔民民俗活动的粗犷豪放，体味渔家风味小吃的原汁原味。

Experience the ruggedness of fishermen's folk activities, and appreciate the original flavor of fisherman's delicacies.

图2

第一课 渔民号子
Lesson 1 Fishermen's Song

长岛的渔民号子,是千百年来,渔民在闯海打鱼的各项劳动中,逐步形成的一种伴随劳动的歌唱。是渔民长期从事海上劳动而创造的歌。它既有鼓舞情绪,调节精神的作用,又有指挥生产,协调动作的功能。渔民说,号子像军号,似命令。喊起它,就来了精神,添了力气;唱着它,能卡着拍子使齐劲,一门心思干活计。这正是它一直常唱不衰,不断创新发展,广泛流传的原因。

The fishermen's song of Changdao is a kind of singing accompanied by labor that has been gradually formed during the various labors of fishermen in rushing into the sea for thousands of years. It is a song created by fishermen who have been engaged in sea labor for a long time. It not only has the function of inspiring emotions and regulating the spirit, but also has the function of directing production and coordinating movements. The fishermen said that the song is like a bugle, like a command. Singing it will give you energy and strength; singing it, you can stick to the beat and work together, and work in one mind. This is the reason why it has been constantly sung, innovated, developed, and spread widely.

渔民号子,有着强烈的生活气息。以吆喝、呐喊为主要特征,烘托出渔业各项劳动的特点。其音乐的表现特色受劳动强度所制约。劳动强度小、动作幅度不大时,所唱出的号子,多是优美动听,抒情委婉,旋律性强,节奏和缓的曲调,突出了号子调节精神

图 2-1-1 渔民号子

的作用；劳动强度大时，所吆喝的号子，粗犷、豪迈、浑厚有力，而节奏性强，这就突出号子的指挥劳动，统一用劲的功能。在面对狂风恶浪，需要奋力抗争时，则发出了铿锵有力、刚劲浑厚、气吞山河的呐喊。

The fishermen's songs have a strong connection with life. With yelling and shouting as the main features, they highlight the characteristics of various fishery labors. The performance characteristics of the music are restricted by labor intensity. When the labor intensity is small and the movement range is not large, the songs are mostly beautiful, lyrical, melodious, and rhythmic, highlighting the role of the song in regulating the spirit; when the labor intensity is high, the shouting songs are rough, bold, vigorous and powerful, and have a strong rhythm. This highlights the function of songs in commanding labor and unifying effort. In the face of violent winds and waves, when fighting hard is needed, the songs have a loud cry of strength, vigor and anger.

渔民号子的演唱形式，主要是"一领众合"式，还有"二部轮唱式"和齐声及重复演唱的。领唱者称为"号头"，合者为"答号"。"一领众合"是多种形式相结合的演唱。如呼应型、叠置型和综合型等。在变化多样的曲调里，大多数只配唱各种语气词，有的填有简单地表达劳动内容和演唱者心情的词语，有的则即兴配词，尽情发挥。同样一种渔号，不少的渔船都沿袭着自己船的唱词。渔船归港，还没看清渔船，只听到渔号，便可知道"哪个船发财了！""谁家的亲人回来了！"

The singing form of the fishermen's song is mainly the "one leader and the crowd" style, as well as the "two-part round singing style" and unison and repetitive singing. The lead singer is called the "trumpet head", and the ensemble is called the "trumpet responders". "One leader and the crowd" is a combination of multiple forms of singing. Such as echo type, stack type and comprehensive type. In the varied tunes, most of them only sing a variety of tonal particles, some are filled with words that simply express the content of labor and the singer's mood, and some are improvised with words to give full play to. The same kind of fishing horn, many fishing boats follow the lyrics of their own boats. When the fishing boat returns to the port, may be they haven't seen the fishing boat clearly, but only by hearing the fishing horn, can know "which boat has made a fortune!"

"whose relatives are back!"

　　渔号的种类，更是应有尽有。上网的、拾锚的、摇橹的、掌篷的、拔缭的、捕鱼的、竖大桅的等，连拉船、掀船（往水里推船），领号者根据船行的节奏，在船上跳着、舞着，即兴喊出指挥和鼓劲的号声。

There are kinds of fishing horns. for mounting net, anchor picking, swaying, palm-topping, pulling, fishing, masting, etc., even pulling and lifting boats (pushing the boat into the water), and according to the rhythm of the boat, the leader will dance on the ship, improvise trumpets of command and encouragement.

　　长岛的渔号，已制出录音，拍成录相，搬上舞台，走进屏幕。一九八九年，中央电视摄制组，专程到砣矶岛，请部分老渔民，在大风船上，用旧时的生产工具，伴着声声渔号，操作着闯海打鱼的活计，录制成《渔民号子》的音乐片，在中央和地方电视台多次播放。当年荣获全国民间文化二等奖。

The fishing horn on Changdao has already been recorded and made into a video, moved onto the stage, and walked onto the screen. In 1989, the CCTV film crew made a special trip to Tuoji Island, and invited some old fishermen, who use the old production tools on the big windboat, accompanied by the sound of fishing horns, and operate the work required when rushing into the sea and catching fish. The music film "The Fisherman's Song" recorded has been broadcast many times on central and local TV stations and won the second prize of National Folk Culture.

　　渔业生产实现机械化以后，海上笨重艰苦的体力劳动多被机械所替代，但是，各种渔民号子仍在渔民的各项劳动中，延续地演唱着。在长岛的海滩码头、山间村落、广场闹市、学校营区，凡有生产劳动的地方，集体活动的场所，还时时传扬着渔号声声。老人扶着小孩子学步，哼着渔号，妇女爬山干活，唱着渔号；小伙们肩挑人拉，喊着渔号，连小学生们的拔河比赛也叫着渔号齐使劲。长岛的渔民号子，还在显示着它旺盛的生命力。

After the mechanized production of fishery was realized, the heavy and arduous manual labor at sea was mostly replaced by machinery. However, various fishermen's songs are still sung in the fishermen's various labors. On Changdao, beach piers, mountain villages, downtown squares, school camps, where there were production and labor, and collective activities, the sound of fishing horns was still heard from time to time. The old man helped the children to walk, hummed the fishing horn, and the women climbed the mountain to work and sang the fishing horn; the boys carried the people on their shoulders and shouted the fishing horn. Even the primary school students shouted the fishing horn in the tug-of-war competition. The fishermen's song of Long Island was still showing its vigorous vitality.

思考与实践

Thinking and practice:

家号子有什么特点？长岛每年都有渔家号子表演活动，注意观察，描写一篇文章。

What are the characteristics of the family song? Every year on Long Island, there is a fisherman's song performance, pay attention to it, and write an article.

第二课 渔家秧歌
Lesson 2 Fisherman's Yangko

图 2-2-1　渔家秧歌

长山列岛唱秧歌（也叫耍秧歌、扭秧歌）始于 20 世纪初，主要由东北地区传入。也汲取了胶东烟台、蓬莱、黄县等农村秧歌的精华。除有和这些地区相同的舞龙、耍狮子、跑旱船、踩高跷等形式外，更多的是，源于海岛生活，表现渔村生产和风情，具有鲜明"海味"特点的渔村秧歌。

Yangko singing on Changshan Islands (also known as playing Yangko and doing yangko dance) began in the early twentieth century and was mainly introduced from the northeast region. The essence of Yangko in rural areas such as Yantai, Penglai and Huangxian in Jiaodong has also been absorbed. In addition to the same forms of dragon dance, lion playing, dry boat running, and walking on stilts as in these areas, it is more of a fishing village Yangko that originates from island life, expresses the production and customs of the fishing village, and has distinctive "sea flavor" characteristics.

　　长岛秧歌大都是海岛人民生产和生活的再现和美化。渔民闯海打鱼，谋生存，求发展，多扑鱼虾，发家致富是海岛渔家世世代代的美好愿望。他们把理想和行动编织在秧歌里，创造出那热烈、雄浑、多彩的网鱼扑虾的舞蹈秧歌。踏着欢快而有节奏的锣鼓点，舞者身着各样服装，头戴各类面具的"鱼流""虾群"，迎着叠起的"浪峰"，窜着汹涌的"波涛"，灵巧活泼地扭动着，弓身迅疾地跑跳着……，数只双人驾驶的彩船，伴着渔号声，张帆摇橹地追赶着、围堵着。一声

"下网了！"那一张张用色彩浸染的渔网，高高扯起，成捕鱼状，那些鱼流、虾群，跑得快捷，躲得轻巧，左冲右突，上蹿下跳，穿插交错、闪转腾跃，颇有百鱼闹海，一网两船的高产丰收的景象。

Changdao Yangko is mostly the reproduction and beautification of the production and life of the people on the island. Fishermen rush to fish in the sea, for seeking survival and development; catching more fish and shrimp, and making a fortune are the good wishes of generations of island fishermen. They woven their ideals and actions into the Yangko, creating the warm, vigorous and colorful Yangko dance, as if they are catching fishes and shrimps. Stepping on the cheerful and rhythmic rhythm played by gongs and drums, the dancers dressed in various costumes, wearing various masks of "fish flow" and "shrimp group", facing the stacked "waves" and rushing turbulent "waves", twisting dexterously, bowed and swiftly ran and jumped..., several double-piloted colorful boats, accompanied by the sound of fishing horns, chased and blocked with their sails hoisted and the oars propelled. "Get off the net!" The color-dipped fishing nets were pulled up high and turned into a flapping fish shape. Those fish and shrimps ran fast, dodged lightly, rushing from the left to the right, and rushing up and down. Jumping, interspersed, flashing and prancing, and there was quite a sight showing hundreds of fish jumping in the sea and a high-yield harvest allowing the two boats fully loaded by the fish caught in one net.

新中国成立以来，海岛人民不断向海洋开发的深度和广度进军。人工养殖海带、扇贝、海参、鲍鱼等正一浪高过一浪，作为源于生活，表现生活的秧歌，在内容和形式上，也有新的突破和发展。海带丰收季节，那海滩上到处是晾晒海带的渔家妇女。她们那拖、拉、挥、甩的刚劲、优美、俏飒的动作，具有一种非常朴素的自然美和劳动美。富

图 2-2-2　渔家秧歌

有灵感的秧歌编创人员，将这如诗如画的情景，稍事加工，提炼、升华，便创作出

具有一定艺术美的《金带飞舞》的秧歌来。

Since the founding of the People's Republic of China, the people of the islands have continuously marched towards the depth and breadth of ocean development. The artificially cultivation of kelp, scallops, sea cucumbers, abalones, etc. are growing increasingly. As a Yangko that originates from and acts as an expression of life, it also has new breakthroughs and developments in contents and forms. During the kelp harvest season, the drying of kelp by women from fishermen's family can be seen everywhere on the beach. Their dragging, pulling, swinging, and swinging, the vigorous, graceful, and sassy movements, had manifested a very simple beauty of nature and work. The personnel for creation of Yangge were so inspiring, only by slight processing, refining, and sublimating of this picturesque scene, enabled the artistically beautiful "Golden Belt Flying Dance" Yangko to be created.

20世纪80年代以来,长岛的扇贝养殖业空前发展。一大批人家靠养扇贝富了起来,扇贝成了海岛人民心中"富"的象征,美的化身。扇贝秧歌便应运而生。每逢节日喜庆,穿红挂绿的渔家儿女,便成排结队。身披淡红色、咖啡色或是金黄色的硕大的扇贝外壳道具,翻飞飘舞起来。一会儿似彩蝶缓缓飞行;一会儿如银燕起伏腾跃;一会儿像仙女飘然下凡;一会儿若群鸥盘旋嬉戏。那整齐的动作,娴熟的技巧,宏大的阵容,喜庆的气氛,令人眼花缭乱,恍于置身在龙宫仙境之中。

Since the 1980s, the scallop cultivation industry in Changdao has developed unprecedentedly. A large number of people have become rich by raising scallops, and scallops have become a symbol of "richness" and the embodiment of beauty in the hearts of the island people, therefore Scallop Yangko came into being. On festive occasions, the young people from fishermen's family wore in red and green, and were lined up and paired. Wearing a huge scallop shell props of light red, brown or golden yellow and fluttering. For a while, it looked like a colorful butterfly flying slowly; for a while, it was like a silver swallow ups and downs and prancing; for a while, it was like a fairy floating down the earth; for a while, it was like a group of gulls circling and frolicking. That neat movement, skilled technique, grand lineup, festive atmosphere make people feal dazzling, as if they were placed in the fairyland of Dragon Palace.

长岛秧歌，不仅增添着节日的喜庆气氛，给人以艺术和美的享受，还授人以生动的教育，助人以活动健身。每当欢庆节日，组织重大活动，都排练有新教育内容秧歌节目。诸如欢庆"七一""国庆""中央两会"等活动，秧歌队里各色人物，总能演唱出"爱党、爱国"等的新秧歌词。演唱者发自肺腑、观看者心领神会。对于"勤劳致富""孝敬老人""计划生育""拥军优属"等传统内容，多由队中男、女青年，着意装扮，脚踏高跷，手持道具，踏着锣鼓点，扭舞表演。场场演出新内容，年年都有新花样，常演常新，百看不厌。

Changdao Yangko, not only adds a few festive atmosphere, gives people the enjoyment of art and beauty, but also enables people to be educated vividly and helps people to exercise. Whenever we celebrate festivals and organize major events, we will rehearse some Yangko programs with new educational content. For activities such as celebrating "July 1", "National Day", and "the holding of NPC and CPPCC", various participants in the Yangko team can always sing new song lyrics such as "Love the Party and the Country". The singers perform from the depth of their hearts, and the viewers understand tacitly. As for traditional contents such as "Becoming Rich through Hard Work", "Honoring the Elderly", "Family Planning", and "Supporting the Army and Superior Family", it is mostly composed of young men and women who dress deliberately, step on stilts, hold props, and dance in line with the rhythm played by gongs and drung. New contents will be added in each performance, with new tricks every year, and the performance will always be new and never make people feel tired of it.

长岛秧歌的筹备和演出，也有一套程序。进入农历腊月，渔业冬闲后期，修船补网，业已结束，各村的同乐会（新中国成立后叫俱乐部），相继组建起来。编创节目，挑选演员，制作道具，都在积极准备。"辞灶"（腊月二十三）以后，便开始拉场排练。先在村内亮相演出，以求改进完善。

There is also a set of procedures for the preparation and performance of Changdao Yangko. In the twelfth month of the lunar calendar, the late period of slack winter season for the fishing industry, the repairing of boats and nets had already ended, and the funfest (called clubs after the founding of the People's Republic of China) had been formed one after another. The ereation of programs, selection of actors and making of props were all actively prepared. After "Celebrating the annuel leawing of kitchen god" (the 23rd of the twelfth lunar month), rehearsals began. The performance starts in village, for further improvement and perfection.

正月初一，天还不大亮，秧歌队便抓紧化妆集合，在"高照"的引领下，红旗、彩旗猎猎，锣鼓、喇叭声声，数百米长的秧歌大队，浩浩荡荡串出村子，在蜿蜒的山路上，像一条巨大的彩龙，向县、乡政府所在地的秧歌会演场地游去。

On the first day of the first lunar month, the dawn is just breaking and the Yangko team rushed for makeup and gathering. Under the guidance of "Gao Zhao", red flags and colorful flags were whistling, with the sound of gongs, drums and trumpets, the hundreds of meters long Yangko team strung out the village mightily. On the winding mountain road, the team, like a huge colorful dragon, swam to the Yangko performance venue where the county and township governments were located.

秧歌队进场演出，也讲究先来后到。一队秧歌在欢迎的鞭炮声中，开进观众自动围成的场地里，慢慢地绕场一周，各种高招绝技，尽情挥洒显露。一圈舞毕，节目逐个退场。最拿手的一二个"压轴戏"，留在场中，铺开场面后，淋漓畅快地来个专场表演。配唱着"拜年""祝贺"等主题词，算是集体团拜的一种形式。在掌声、笑声、鼓乐声、鞭炮声的欢送中，完成了一个村队的演出。

When the Yangko team entered to show, they also observed the order of entrance. A team of Yangko drove into the arena automatically enclosed by the audience amidst the sound of welcoming firecrackers, slowly circling around the stadium, showing all kinds of masterful tricks. After a lap of dance, the show exited one by one. One or two of the most proficient "final scenes" stayed in the field. After the scenes were spread out, there would be a special performance freely and vividly. Singing with theme words such as "New Year's Greetings" and "Congratulations" is a form of group worship. With applause, laughter, drums, and firecrackers, the performance of a village team was completed.

会演结束，各队或到驻军营区，或走村串疃，尽兴表演，有时，还乘船出岛演出。

At the end of the performance, each team may go to the garrison area, or go to the village to perform. Sometimes, they even take a boat out of the island to perform.

平日的重大喜庆活动,随时组织,爱好和善长者,踊跃参加,近几年每临傍晚时分,海岛的街头巷尾,渔港码头,中老年人,少年儿童,自动组织,踏着录音拍节,摇羽扇,舞彩绸,扭起秧歌,休闲娱乐,活动健身。尽情地享受着长岛秧歌给人们带来的身心健康和艺术享受。

Major festive activities were organized on weekdays at any time. People who are fond of and good at them have presented active participation. In recent years, every evening, in the streets and lanes of the island, and the fishing port, the middle-aged and the elderly, the young and children, are automatically organized, stepping on the recording beat, shaking the feather fan, waving color silk, and doing the Yangko dance, realizing leisure and entertainment, exercise and fitness. Enjoying the physical and mental health and feeling the artistic enjoyment that Changdao Yangko brings to people.

思考与实践

Thinking and practice

渔家大秧歌有什么特点? 你观看过大秧歌表演了吗,谈谈你的感受。

What are the characteristics of fishermen's Yangko? Have you watched the big Yangko performance? Talk about your feelings.

第三课　赶庙会
Lesson 3　Temple Fair

图 2-3-1　拜妈祖

图 2-3-2　拜妈祖

参拜显应宫庙，祭祷天后圣母，是渔民船家世世代代神圣虔诚的传统活动，千百年来，显应宫神连四海，灵结五洲，拜谒者络绎不绝，香火长年不断。根据庙史资料记载：最晚到道光年间，以显应宫为中心的庙岛群岛海域，成为当时黄、渤海地区的第一大锚泊港口。南涯（奥、闽、江、淮一带）北邦（辽、津、营口、丹东等地和胶东诸地）的官、商、渔、漕等各种船只，均以此地为中继和货物的集散地，成为南北洋物资交流的中心，每年农历七月十五日前后，各商会、船帮，聚首庙岛报关上税，举办盂兰盆会，敬请天下南、北腔各名班在庙岛搭台唱戏。最多时搭戏棚达四、五十座，各班有的要同时作场，竞相献艺。时间长者，一月有余。一时间，"商贾云集、阜物如山"，各地客商纷纷到此赶会，买卖百货。各类船只增补给养，拜庙祭神。船舶集散往来，桅杆竞数以万计。当时，有这样的诗句："帆樯林立往来不绝，笙歌燕舞通宵达旦"。可见，当时拜庙赶会的盛景。

Visiting the Xianying Temple and praying to the Lady of God are regarded as sacred and pious traditional activities for generations of fishermen. For thousands of years, the Xianying Temple has been worshipped by all of the world. There is an endless stream of worshippers and incense is kept constantly throughout the year. According to the historical records of temples, during the Daoguang period of Qing Dynasty at the latest, the waters of the Miaodao Islands with Xianying Temple as the center became the largest anchor port in the Huanghai and Bohai Seas at that time. Beibang, from the southern part (Ao, Min, Jiang, Huai area) and northern part (Liao, Jin, Yingkou, Dandong and other places and Jiaodong places), all kinds of ships, including officials, merchants, fishing, and water transport of grain, all use this place as a relay and the distribution center of the goods which has also become the center for the exchange of materials between the North and the South. Around the 15th day of the lunar calendar every year, various ships from chambers of commerce and shipping organizations gathered here for customs declaration and taxation, and the Bon Festival was theatrical troupes from the northern and southern part were invited, for setting up a stage to sing on the Island. At most, forty to fifty tents for playing are set up, and some of the troupes had to perform at the same time and competed to perform. The longest time for performance was more than one month. For a time, "merchants gathered, and things were like mountains." Merchants from all over the county came here to rush to meet, buy and sell goods. All kinds of ships added supplies, and worshiped temples and gods. Ships gathered here, and tens of thousands of masts can be seen. At that time, there was such a verse: "The sails are endless, singing and dancing all night long." It can be seen that the scene of worshipping the temple at that time was so spectacular.

随着陆上交通的发展,烟台等地的开埠建港,长岛的海运逐渐萧条。庙岛的孟兰庙会便不再那么风光兴盛了。但是,长山列岛及胶东沿海各地的船家渔民仍时时祭典神庙,拜谒天后圣母,希冀圣母神佑荫护。想要祛病消灾的,求子祈福的,保佑平安的,祷告发财的,从未间断;凡诸如愿者,均拜叩神祇,进香敬谢,奉礼还愿,捐金修庙塑像者,也时而有之。人来客往,车水马龙。虽然随时方便,但终不成规模,不便于交流观摩,推动提高。人们需要有固定的拜庙祭神的统一时间,自然地选择了渔、农冬闲的春节后第一大节——元宵节。这就形成了元宵节庙岛显应宫庙会的民俗活动。

With the development of land transportation and the opening of ports in Yantai and other places, the shipping of Changdao became depressed gradually. The Yulan Temple Fair on the Island is no longer prosperous. However, the fishermen of the Changshan Islands and the coastal areas of Jiaodong still worship the temples from time to time and pay homage to the Goddess, hoping for her protection, Ceaseless flow of people come here for worship, including those who want to cure illnesses and disasters, pray for children, peace, and wealth; those who realize their wish will worship the gods, offer incense and give thanks, reciprocate vows, and donate gold to build statues in the temple occasionally. People come and go, with many vehicles. Although it is convenient at any time, no scale would be formed in the end, and it is not applicable for exchanges, observations or further improvement. People need a fixed time for worshiping the temple and the gods, so they naturally choose the first major festival after the Spring Festival, the Lantern Festival, after fishing, farming and winter leisure period. This formed the folklore activities of the Xianying Temple Fair in Island during Lantern Festive.

春节刚过，欢庆的海岛渔家，兴犹未尽，十五元宵节又将来临。忆旧岁，得福发财的、遇难呈祥的；望新年，祈求保佑的，期望丰收的，人们揣着各种各样的心情，怀着无限美好的愿望，忙碌着敬神的祭品，准备那赶庙会的节目，要在庙会上奉献虔诚之心，大显欢庆的身手绝技。

Just after the Spring Festival, the rejoice of island fishermen still linger, and the Lantern Festival would come again. Recalling the old days, those who are blessed and wealthy, those survive from disasters; looking forward to the New Year, those who pray for blessings, and those who look forward to a good harvest, all kinds of moods and infinitely beautiful wishes make people busy with godly sacrifices, and prepare for the show to be performed in the temple fair. We must devote ourselves to the temple fair and show off the skill for celebration.

长岛的世代渔家，一向甘为人先，许多事要争个头彩。行船，要一帆风顺，第一个到达；生产要创最高产量，争个头名；拜庙敬神，也要抢在前面，早早表达敬意，献上神礼，早得圣母的垂爱。期望娘娘保佑，在新的一年里，出门早发财，好事诸在先。在邻近海岛渔村的，"近水楼台"，先拜为荣。看护神庙者尚未起床，庙门外便响起了鞭炮声。那远在百里之外的北五岛的渔家，也要"捷足快登"，不甘人后。他们以渔为主，实现机械化以后，争先赶庙会的愿望，仍可实现。正月十五日的凌晨，这边的庙会尚未揭幕，海上的"龙舟大赛"便已开始。经过冬季坞修一新的渔轮，千机轰鸣，百舸争流。大、小红吊子，小角旗、各色彩旗，迎风劲舞，新油漆的渔轮，张贴着大红的春联。船头犁蹚着碧波万顷，船边翻滚白浪长龙，加足马力，你追我赶，向仙岛神祇飞驰。多好的一幅美丽壮观海上赶会的彩卷啊！

The generations of fishermen in Changdao have always been willing to be the first. Sailing must be smooth and the first to arrive. They must achieve the highest yield in production, worship the temple and the gods ahead of the time, express respect early, offer divine salutes, and receive the love from early. They hope to be blessed. and In the new year, go out and make a fortune early, and good things come first. In the nearby fishing villages on the islands, people are proud of their corvenient access for worship. Before the guardian of the temple got up, firecrackers sounded outside the temple gate. The fishermen on the North Five Islands, which are hundreds of miles away, will also "catch up quickly", and are unwilling to be left behind. Their main focus is on fishing, and their desire to rush to the temple fair after mechanization can still be realized. In the early morning of the 15th of the first lunar month, the temple fair here has not yet been unveiled, and the "dragon boat race" on the sea has already begun. The vessel repaired on dock during winter is refreshed. Big and little red hangings, small horn flags, flags of various colors were waved in the wind; freshly painted fishing boats are put up with red spring festival couplets. The bow plow is wading through the blue waves. The water waves roll along the boat. People add enough horsepower, chase each other, and gallop towards the god of the fairy island. What a beautiful and magnificent color scroll for a meeting on the sea.

南五乡镇的各类公、私客船，全部开动，皆免费接送拜庙赶会的乘客。船来客往，穿梭般地忙碌不停，多装快运，向神庙圣母多献一份份虔诚。

All types of public and private passenger ships in the southern five townships are in operation, and they are all free to take passengers who worship temples and banquets. The boats come and go, shuttle busily without stop, allow more to be loaded and run faster, offering more piety to the Virgin of the Temple.

珍珠门外,船流还在涌动;庙岛塘内,客船仍忙碌未停。庙岛这边,赶会的人们,一拨接一拨,一群连一群,早已上香拜娘娘了。整个神庙院落,鞭炮齐鸣,烟飞纸舞,香火缭绕,钟声阵阵。熙熙攘攘的前院、各庙殿、后宫,人们摩肩接踵,祈祷声声。观瞻了兵帅将军、海神龙王,再膜拜天后圣母。接着便是敬献神礼:娘娘的各类塑像、各样的匾额条幅,仿制的船模,圣母的衣物服饰,日常用品,应有尽有,而且无不精心制作,巧夺天工。走进东西廊房,饶有兴致地参观各个展室。中国造船史、海运史、航海技术史、海上兵事史和郑和纪念馆、妈祖史迹馆等。最近几年,又新增了海岛民间手工艺品和书画作品展,吸引着赶会的人们驻足忘返。

Outside the Pearl Gate, the flow of ships was still surging. Inside the island pond, the passenger ships were still running busily. On the island, the people rushed to the meeting, one after another, and had already gone to the incense to worship the empress. Throughout the temple courtyard, firecrackers sounded, smoke flew paper danced, incense wafted, and bells rang. In the bustling front yard, people gathered and prayed in the temples, and harems. They watched General, Sea God Dragon King, and worshipped the Queen Mother. Then there was the dedication ceremony, various statues of the empress, plaques and banners, imitated ship models, the clothes of the Goddess, daily necessities, everything, and all of them were carefully crafted and ingenious. Walking into the east and west gallery room and visiting the exhibition rooms with great interest, such as China's shipbuilding history, maritime history, maritime technology history, maritime military history, Zheng He Memorial Hall, Mazu Historical Sites, etc. In recent years, an exhibition of island folk handicrafts, calligraphy and painting had been added, attracting people who rushed to the meeting, and they would stop here and forget to return.

赶庙会,还有一项神圣的活动,是敲钟祈福。在东边的钟楼下,人们怀着各样美好的愿望,在心中默默地祈祷着,手持钟槌,摇动连敲。敲三下,连中三元,学业有成;撞六响,六六大顺,万事如意;击九声,九九高寿,幸福安康。

There was also a sacred event in the temple fair, ringing the bell to pray for blessings. Under the bell tower on the east side, people prayed silently in their hearts with all kinds of good wishes, holding the bell mallet, shaking and knocking. Knocking three times, representing getting three highest literary degrees in success, and succeding in academic. Hitting six times meant good luck, and everything going well. Hitting nine times meant longevity, happiness and well-being.

九时许，庙会进入高潮，集体庆典开始。鼓乐阵阵，人声鼎沸，数以万计的妈祖信徒在"力挽狂澜"牌坊下的广场上，观看庙会节目。金龙腾飞，彩狮劲舞，频频向神庙圣母叩首参拜；人们踩着高跷，欢快表演，寓意着海岛人民高抬双足，翘望未来，致富建岛的美好愿望；渔民号子，再现了长岛渔民凝聚力量，统一动作，战风斗浪，气吞山河的闯海人形象；驻军战士的锣鼓表演，气势宏伟，威风八面，敲浓了军民鱼水深情，敲定了守卫宝岛，建设第二故乡的决心；众多的秧歌队里，有近两年新增的海珍品活报剧。那"鲍鱼""海参""海胆""虾夷贝"等的表演，生动逼真，活灵活现，表达了长岛人民调整产业结构，实现养殖生产第三次飞跃的目标和信心。

At about nine o'clock, the temple fair reached its climax and the collective celebration began. With drums and vocals, tens of thousands of Mazu followers watched the temple fair on the square under the memorial archway embodying "Turn The Tide". The golden dragon soared, the colorful lion danced vigorously, and frequently kowtowed to the Goddess. People stepped on stilts and performed cheerfully, implying the good wishes of the people of the island to, looking forward to the future, and becoming rich and building the island. The chant of the fishermen reproduced the image of the sea strivers, gathering strength, unifying actions, fighting the wind and waves, and being full of dares. The gongs and drums performances by the garrison soldiers were magnificent and majestic, which made the soldiers and civilians affectionate, and finalized the determination to guard the treasure island and build the second hometown. Among many Yangko teams, there were sea treasures dramas newly added in the past two years. The performances of abalone, sea cucumber, sea urchin and shrimp scallop were vivid, expressing the goal and confidence of the people of Changdao to adjust the industrial structure and realize the third leap of aquaculture production.

广场文化活动结束以后，各专业文艺队伍，外地进岛的艺术团体，便在神庙的大、小戏楼，临时搭起的舞台上，争相演出，赤诚献艺……。

After the cultural activities in the square ended, various professional art teams and the groups coming from other places, rushed to perform in the temporary stages in the large and small theaters of the temple.

一天的庙会，人们叩谒天后圣母，进香膜拜，还了许愿，留下了祈祷，捐了香火钱，敬献了一份份虔诚，寄托着美好的希望，满意而归。

At the one-day temple fair, people greeted the Goddess, worshipped with incense, made a wish, left prays, donated money for incense, offered a share of piety, placed good hopes, and returned with satisfaction.

思考与实践

Thinking and practice

长岛每年什么时候举办庙会？你参加过吗？谈谈你的感受。

When does Changdao hold temple fairs every year? Have you participated? Talk about your feelings.

第四课　鲅鱼　水饺　鲜鱼面　海菜包子

Lesson 4　Spanish mackerel dumplings, fresh fish noodles and sea vegetables steamed buns

鲅鱼水饺
Spanish mackerel dumplings

鱼馅水饺是长岛人最常见的海鲜小吃。黄花鱼、牙鲆鱼、鲳鱼、鲈鱼等的鱼肉馅水饺已属上乘,但最经济实惠,颇具特色的当推鲅鱼馅水饺。

Fish dumplings are the most common seafood snack for Changdao people. Fish dumplings such as yellow croaker, flounder, pomfret, sea bass, etc. are already excellent, but the most economical and distinctive dumplings are mackerel dumplings.

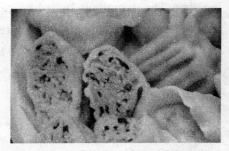

图 2-4-1　海菜包子

鱼水饺的口味如何,关键在调馅。俗话说:"拌好饺子馅,撑死大肚汉。"将一斤以上的新鲜鲅鱼,让头去骨,片下两片鱼肉,再剔除鱼皮和皮下的红肉,把白肉切成小块,放入适量的精盐、葱花、姜末等调料。调馅时,一边加水,一边搅拌,直搅得鱼块全部粉碎,成稠糊状,挑出一撮,稍能成堆,加进切细的韭菜。(用春夏季的嫩葱白做配料,那便有另一番风味。)

The key to the taste of fish dumplings is mixing of stuffing. As the saying goes: "The dumplings stuffing mixed well can make the big belly man to be stuffed." Removing the bones and head from fresh spanish mackerel, of more than half kilometer slicing two pieces of fish, then removing the skin and the red meat under the skin, and cutting the white meat into small pieces. Adding appropriate amount of salt, chopped green onion, bruised ginger and other seasonings. During mixing, adding water while stirring until the fish pieces are crushed into a thick paste. Picking out some paste and forming a pile, and adding the finely chopped leeks. (If scallions picked in spring and summer are used as ingredients, then there will be another flavor.)

饺子的包法也有讲究,面团要揉到数；皮儿杆得精薄,几乎要透出馅来；馅子放得特多,勉强能够捏住饺子边；饺子包得老大。大锅急火,煮出来的饺子,晶薄剔透的皮内,饱含着白绿相间的肉蛋,像裹着一层薄皮的大鱼丸子。咬一口鲜嫩清新,香而不腻,仿佛有鲜汤香汁要从口角边流出,回味无穷。

The method of making dumplings is also exquisite. The dough has to be kneaded enough. The skin is made thin enough to reveal their sluffing almost. Too much stuffing is wrapped, in this way the wrapper is relutant to be pinched logether. The dumplings boiled by cauldron and intense fine show crystal clear wrapper, inside of which is the white-green mixtuce of meat and egg, just like a fish ball wrapped with a thin skin. It tastes fresh, fragrant but not greasy, as if there is a fresh soup and fragrant juice coming out of the corner of the mouth, with endless aftertaste.

鲜鱼面
Fresh Fish Noodle

图 2-4-2　鲜鱼面

长岛的鲜鱼面,是指混汤面(也叫大面、白吃面)一般的做法是,热锅加油烧开,放葱、蒜爆锅后,倒进鲜鱼块,稍加爆炒,添水浇开,把擀好的面条丢入锅中,煮熟加青头(韭菜、菠菜、香菜等)。鲜嫩的鱼块,滑溜的面条和新鲜青菜,白汁混汤,色、香、味俱佳。

Changdao' s fresh fish noodles refer to mixed noodles (also called big noodles and white noodles). The general cooking method is to heat up a pan with oil until boiling, add green onions and garlic to the pan, pour the fresh fish pieces into it, and stir-fry for a while. Adding water until boiling, throwing the well rolled noodles into the pot, cooking and adding green vegetables (leeks, spinach, coriander, etc.). Fresh and tender fish, slippery noodles and fresh green vegetables as well as good white sauce and mixed soup result in the color, fragrance and taste.

鲜鲐鱼面，要配加细玉米面，才有独特风味。将鲜鲐鱼块，稍加精盐卤渍，沥去卤水，鱼块稍微干缩。稍硬的面团，揉匀手擀，切成三寸余的短条。煮成的鱼面，鱼块稍硬而不破碎，清鲜利索，鲜中微咸；面条硬挣爽口，有咬嚼；面汤略浑而鲜香味特别，是鲜鱼面之最。

Fresh mackerel noodles must be served with fine corn noodles to have a unique flavor. Making fresh mackerel cubes added with a little bit of brine, draining off the brine, and shrinking the fish cubes slightly. Kneading the slightly harder dough, rolling it out by hand, and cutting into short strips of more than three inches. In the boiled fish noodles, the fish pieces are slightly hard but not broken, fresh and crisp, and slightly salty in the freshness, the noodles are hard and refreshing, and a bit chewy; the noodle soup is slightly muddy and fragrant, which is the most fresh fish noodle.

海菜包子
Steamed Buns with Sea Vegetable Stuffing

以海菜做包子，长岛人称之为海菜夹子（也有叫菜角子）。长岛一年四季均有时新海菜，可做包子的用菜。海青菜、紫菜、铜藻、裙带菜、鹿角菜等，诸菜中当属早春的骆驼毛（萱菜）菜做包子最多见。每年的二月以后，海边礁石上生长出的骆驼毛，呈深褐色、纤细、柔嫩、光滑。落潮时，赶海捞菜，平礁上的短菜，用鲍鱼壳刮，稍长的用手捋，浅水里的往上捞。

图 2-4-3　海菜包子

To make steamed buns with sea vegetables, the people of Changdao call them sea vegetables clips (also called Caijiaozi). There are fresh sea vegetables in Changdao all year round, which can be used for steamed buns. Sea green vegetables, seaweed, copper algae, wakame, carrageenan, etc., among the various dishes, camel camel hair (Xuan Cai), which grows in early spring is most commonly used for bun. After February each year, the camel hair (name of vegetable) that grows on the seaside reef is dark brown, slender, tender and smooth. When the tide is low, the vegetables are obtained from the sea, scraping the short vegetables on the flat meat with abalone shells, tapping the longer ones with your hands, and fishing up the ones in shallow water.

海菜一般都喜大油和大蒜。所以岛上人做海菜包子时,除用足食油外,多用肉丁和大蒜片配馅。包子的皮以烫面为好,个头不大,但菜要塞实包严。蒸熟以后,尚未揭锅,鲜香味便扑鼻而来。咬一口稀溜滑润,清鲜可口,总有肚子饱了眼不饱的感觉。

Sea vegetables tend to be cooked together with oil and garlic. Therefore, when people on the island make seaweed buns, in addition to using enough cooking oil, they often use diced meat and garlic slices as fillings. The skin of the buns is better made of the dough knedded with hot water. They are not big, but sealed tightly. After being steamed, the fresh fragrance will come out without uncovering the pot; you will feal smooth, fresh and delicious by taking a bit of it, and you will always be eager to eat more, even if you are full.

思考与实践

Thinking and practice
与家长合作,尝试做一做,品尝后谈谈感受。
Cooperate with parents, try to do it, and talk about your feelings after tasting.

第五课　饼子咸鱼鲜鱼丸子"哈"海蜇

Lesson 5　Pancakes Combined Salted Fish, Fresh Fish Balls and "Ha" Jellyfish

饼子咸鱼
Pancake Salted Fish

现在,生活水平提高了,山珍海味均可吃到。但要吃到长岛正宗的饼子咸鱼,并非易事。

Now, the living standard has improved, and you can eat many delicacies. But it is not easy to eat the authentic pancakes cimbined salted fish in Changdao.

图 2-5-1　饼子咸鱼

玉米面里要掺和适量的黄豆面,加稍热水调和得不软不硬,锅热时,把和好的饼子面团,在手中反复弹拍,摔拍在锅边近水处(叫糊饼子),草火快烧。糊出来淡黄色的饼子,香喷喷的,用手掂掂,轻生生的,拍一拍,嘭嘭有声,吃在嘴里,暄噗噗的,香中略带一丝甜味。那饼子骼,焦黄酥脆,吃起来,比饼子又强几分。

The cornmeal should be mixed with an appropriate amount of soybean noodles, adding a little hot water to make it blended properly. When the pan is hot, pat the mixed pancake dough repeatedly in your hands near the water near at the edge of the pan (called mashed pancake), the grass is burnt fast. The light yellow pancakes are fragrant, you will feel a little bit light when make it weighed in your hand; a popping sound will be heard when you pat it; besider, it tastes to be soft, fragrant and a little sweet. The pancake bones, browned and crispy, taste better than pancakes.

上讲究的咸鱼有三种：春鲐、秋鲅、夏瓜板（高眼鲽又名"长脖）。

春天进湾繁殖的鲐鱼体肥个大。整鱼洗净后，从头顺脊背剖开，只摘除内脏，冲洗鱼腹中的血污。在坛子里，撒一层底盐，将鲐鱼的剖面朝上摆平，再撒一层盐，再放一层鱼，最后再盖一层盐，然后用干净的扁石等压住。汁流盐化，汤浸过鱼，待鱼和汤发蒸过来，捞出蒸熟。原汁原味，吃在嘴里越咀嚼越有味。难怪有"箱一筷子九咂摸，一条鱼吃短了三双筷子"的夸张说法。

There are three types of salted fish that are exquisite: spring mackerel, autumn mackerel, and summer squash plate (Cleithenes herzensteini also called "long neck").

The mackerel that breeds in the bay in spring is fat and big. After the whole fish is washed, it is cut open from the head and the back, only the internal organs are removed, and the blood in the abdomen of the fish is washed. In the jar, sprinkle a layer of salt on the bottom flatten the cross section of the mackerel, sprinkle another layer of salt, put another layer of fish, and finally cover it with a layer of salt, and then press it with a clean flat stone. The juice is salted, and the fish is soaked in the soup. When the fish and the soup are steamed, make it removed and steamed. The original taste makes you feel more delicious in the mouth. It is no wonder that its delicious and fragrant taste is more exaggerated.

深秋的鲅鱼，最肥鲜，皮下和骨缝都长了油脂。选个大的，从脊背剖开，剔除内脏，横切数段，撒大盐腌渍。要吃时，放在凉水中，浸泡得稍有咸味，切成条状，加葱花、姜末蒸熟。吃起来，鲜味不减，咸度不大，香味特别。

Spanish mackerel in late autumn is the fattest and freshest, with grease growing under the skin and between the bones. Choose a large one, cut it open from the back, remove the internal organs, cut several sections across, and sprinkle a large amount of salt for pickling. When you want to eat, put it in cold water, soak it for a slightly salty taste, cut into strips, add chopped green onion and ginger to steam. When being tasted, the umami taste is not diminished, the saltiness is not big, and the fragrance is special.

初夏淡盐晒干瓜板鱼，捂放一段时间。蒸熟后，鱼肉会脱骨离刺，散成微干面软的鱼片，就着热饼子，那真是不可多得的美味，连鱼的骨刺都酥软，吃嚼起来，特有味道。

In early summer, drying the squash with light salt and keep it for a period of time. After being steamed, the fish will be separated from its bones and spurs;when eated together with hot pancake, you'll feel it rarely delicious. Even the bones of the fish are soft and chewy, it has an unique taste.

鲜鱼丸子
Fresh fish balls

每当鲜鱼上市，岛上人总喜欢吃顿鲜鱼丸子。不仅鲅鱼、鲐鱼、牙鲆鱼、鲳鱼等可做丸子，就连那鱼小刺多的鲫鱼、小黄肚、大头宝等也尽可做成。其做法与调鱼饺子馅基本相同。只是那些小鱼，要摘头去骨，不用剔刺，放在菜板上剁得精细即可。

图2-5-2　鲜鱼丸子

Whenever fresh fish is on the market, people on the island always like to eat fresh fish balls. Not only Spanish mackerel, mackerel, flounder, pomfret, etc. can be made into meatballs, but also crucian carp, xiao huang du, Da tou bao, etc. with many small spines. The cooking method is basically the same as that of fish dumpling filling. Just , you need to remove the head and the bone of those small fish, without need to pick out fish bones, just chop finely on the cutting board.

长岛人做鱼丸也有特点。妇女在家里，一般都是先把水烧个七八成开，将鱼馅放在手里，待手掌一握，一个圆滑的鱼丸子便从拇指和食指圈成的圆孔中"扑登"一声掉进水锅里，这样一张一合，动作很是麻利。下出的丸子，雪白、鲜嫩、晶莹如珠。当地称为"攥丸子"。

People in Changdao also have their own characteristics in cooking fish balls. At home, women usually select the water no fully boiled, put the fish stuffings in their hands, and when they hold a smooth fish ball in their palms, they will make it slide down from the circular hole formed by the thumb and index finger, and falling into the water pot, and the above action is repeated quickly. The balls that come out are snow-white, tender, and crystal clear like beads. It is known as "balls cooking".

渔民在海上生产,吃鱼丸子便没有这般斯文、仔细。待鱼肉剁细调拌好后,干脆操起勺子将馅子一下一下往开水锅里挖。这样煮熟后,一碗也只能盛二三个,人们称之为"挖鱼丸子"。吃着鲜嫩的鱼肉丸子,喝着热鲜汤,别有一番风味。

During fishing on the sea, fishermen are not so gentle and careful when they eat fish balls. After the fish is finely chopped and mixed, simply use a spoon to dig the stuffing into the boiling water pot. After being cooked in this way, only two or three can be carried in one bowl, which was called "digging fish balls". It is a special flavor to eat fresh and tender fish meatballs and drink hot soup.

"哈" 海蜇
"Ha" jellyfish

海蜇(水母)皮拌凉菜,是一般人都熟悉的吃法。在长岛还有一种独特的海味,名曰"哈"海蜇。

Cold dish with jellyfish skin is a familiar way of eating. There is also a unique seafood in Changdao called "Ha" jellyfish.

岛上人管"喝"叫"哈"。夏、秋季是海蜇旺汛,岛上人把打捞上来的海蜇,除去头爪,切大块放入水里浸泡。要"哈"时,先用刀将海蜇削成片状,再如切面条般地将其切匀切细,然后用清水冲洗几遍,除净咸腥味。再适量地加入精盐、香油、味精、食醋、香菜、辣椒等调料。诸料配好拌匀,便可开怀畅"哈"了。那海蜇条清亮如水,滑溜溜,凉渍渍,辣苏苏的,嘴嚼起来,格嘣嘣,脆生生的,直撩气拨人的胃口,诱着你喝完一碗,还想再喝。"哈"海蜇所用的调料,因人的口味嗜好而各异。岛上还有一种糖拌的"哈"海蜇,那

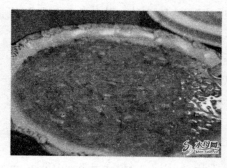

图2-5-2 鲜鱼丸子

又是一番风味。

People on the island call "drinking" to be "ha". Summer and autumn are jellyfish flourishing seasons. People on the island remove the head and claws of the salvaged jellyfish, cut them into large pieces, and soak them in water. When you want to "ha", firstly using a knife to cut the jellyfish into slices, then cut it evenly and finely like noodles, then rinsing it with water for several times to remove the salty smell. Then add salt, sesame oil, monosodium glutamate, vinegar, coriander, chili and other seasonings in an appropriate amount. The ingredients are mixed well, and you can "ha" cheerfully. The jellyfish sticks are as clear as water, slippery, pleasantly cool, spicy, chewing, crunchy, and irritating people's appetite, tempting to drink one after another. The seasoning used in "Ha" jellyfish varies with people's tastes. There is also a kind of "ha" jellyfish mixed with sugar on the island, which is another flavor.

思考与实践

Thinking and practice

与家长合作，尝试做一做，品尝后谈谈感受。

Cooperate with parents, try to do it, and talk about your feelings after tasting.

第三单元　地方特产

Unit 3　Local Specialties

长岛是中国鲍鱼、海带之乡,海珍品扬名海内外;长岛球石、砣矶砚石名扬四海。

Changdao is the hometown of abalone and kelp in China, and its sea treasures are well-known at home and abroad; Changdao ball stone and Tuoji inkstone are well-known all over the world.

第一课 鲍鱼刺参对虾海胆

Lesson 1 Abalone, Sea Cucumber, Prawn, Sea Urchin

皱纹盘鲍
Wrinkled Abalone

鲍鱼是一种珍贵的贝类。它壳形似耳，单面，内装蘑菇状的肉体（大部分为鲍鱼吸足），吸附在礁岩砾石上，爬动觅食。

Abalone is a precious shellfish. Its shell is similar to ears, single-sided, and contains mushroom-like flesh (most of which is abalone sucking feet), which is adsorbed on the reef gravel and crawls for food.

图 3-1-1 皱纹盘鲍

长岛县砣矶以北，海水清澈，水深流急，礁石岩洞密布，海藻饵料丰富，最适宜鲍鱼生长、繁殖。所产的皱纹盘鲍，个体肥大，肉质细嫩，味道鲜美，营养丰富，被誉为海珍品之冠。可做成"红烧鲍鱼""扒鲍鱼"等名菜。在长岛则多以鲜蒸鲍鱼上桌，原汁原味，鲜美无比。

To the north of Tuoji, Changdao County, the sea is clear, the water is deep and rapid, the reefs are densely covered with caves, and the seaweed is rich in bait, which is the most suitable for abalone is growth and reproduction. The wrinkled abalone grown here is fat, tender, delicious and nutritious, and is known as the crown of sea treasures. It can be made into famous dishes such as "Braised Abalone" and "Grilled Abalone". In Changdao, fresh steamed abalone is always served on the table, which is original and delicious.

　　鲍鱼浑身是宝，其肉具去腐生肌作用，食之对手术后，收敛伤口，软化肌肤，减小疤痕，有显著效果。其壳即石决明，是名贵中药材，可治高血压和眼疾等。

Abalone is full of treasures; its meat has the effect of decomposing and regenerating muscles, which is conducive to pestoperative recovery, such as tightening wounds, softening the skin and reducing scars, and a significant effect can be obtained. Its shell is cassia stone, which is a precious Chinese medicinal material and can be used to treat high blood pressure and eye diseases.

刺参
Sea Cucumber

　　海参属棘皮动物，种类很多。胶东半岛和辽东半岛沿海产的刺参属优良品种。长岛产的刺参品质最佳。加工后，肉体肥厚、硬实，营养丰富。深受行家们的赏识。外地也多有贩卖者盗名假冒而售之。

Sea cucumbers belong to echinoderms, and varied in types. The sea cucumbers from the coastal areas of Jiaodong Peninsula and Liaodong Peninsula are excellent varieties. The sea cucumber from Changdao has the best quality. After processing, the flesh is thick, firm, and nutritious. It is well received by connoisseurs. There are also many vendors in other places who sell them by stealing their names.

图 3-1-2　长岛刺参

　　刺参是名贵的滋补品，为山珍海味之一。干品含蛋白质 70% 以上，并含有钙、磷、铁、碘等多种对人体有益成分，具有补肾壮阳、益气补阴、通肠润肺作用。是公认的冬补最佳食品。年老、体弱、病伤者食用，有显著的延缓衰老，强健体魄、祛病养伤的功效。做成菜肴则是宴会上的名菜，吃法有"大扒海参""红烧海参""烩海参""拌打参丝"等。

Sea cucumber is a valuable tonic, and regarded as one of the delicacies. The dry product contains more than 70% protein, and also calcium, phosphorus, iron, iodine and other components beneficial to the human body. It is recognized as the best food for winter tonic. It can be eaten by the elderly, weak, and injured, which has significant effects of delaying aging, strengthening the body, and healing the wounds. They are the famous dishes at the banquet, and they can be eaten with "big grilled sea cucumber", "broiled sea cucumber", "braised sea cucumber", "mixed shredded sea cucumber" and so on.

长岛海域适合刺参生长。历史上资源丰富,产量平均每年达 6 吨以上 (干品)。20 世纪 80 年代开始实行人工增养,每年向海区投放大批海参苗。近年又开始人工建池养殖。

The waters of Changdao are suitable for the growth of sea cucumbers. Historically, the resources are abundant, with an average annual output of more than 6 tons (dry products). Artificial feeding began in the 1980s, and a large number of sea cucumber seedlings were put into the sea every year. In recent years, artificial pond farming has begun.

对虾
Prawns

对虾 (又名大虾、明虾、闽虾),因过去常成对出售而得名。是名贵海产品之一,主要分布于黄、渤海。长岛周围海域是其"生殖洄游"与"越冬洄游"必经之地,也是我国北方捕虾的主要渔场。

图 3-1-3 渤海湾对虾

Prawns are so named because they were often sold in pairs in the past. As one of the precious seafood, The prauns are mainly distributed in the Yellow Sea and Bohai. The waters around Changdao are the only way for their "reproductive migration" and "overwintering migration", and also the main fishing ground for shrimp fishing in northern part of China.

对虾肉味道鲜美,营养丰富,每百克含蛋白质 20.6 克,含脂肪 0.7 克,并含钙、磷、铁等元素与多种维生素,为高级宴席上不可缺少的佳肴。我国产的对虾是世界三大名虾之一,具有很高的经济价值,许多国家都以高昂的价格争相进口,过去一直是我国出口创汇的重要产品,在国内销售价格也很高。

The prawn tastes delicious and nutritious. It contains 20.6 grams of protein and 0.7 grams of fat per 100 grams, and also calcium, phosphorus, iron and other elements, as well as multiple vitamins. It is an indispensable delicacy for high-end banquets. The prawns produced in China are one of the world's three famous shrimps and have high economic value. Many countries are vying to import them at high prices. In the past, they have always been important products for my country's export and foreign exchange earning, and also sold at higher prices domestically.

对虾鲜食法有烹虾段、炸虾球、溜虾片、氽汤等,长岛人喜欢用虾肉、猪肉、韭菜和馅制作"三鲜饺子",其味鲜美无比。除鲜食外,也可制虾干、钳籽米等干品。

Fresh prawns can be cooked as follows, including cooked prawns, fried prawn balls, prawn slices, and soup. Islanders like to make "three fresh dumplings", with prawns, pork and leeks used as stuffing, which are extremely delicious. In addition to fresh food, dried shrimps, pincer rice and other dried products can also be made.

光棘球海胆
Strongylocentrotus nudus

图 3-1-4 皱纹盘鲍

海胆属棘皮动物门的海胆纲。品种很多。长岛产的光棘球海胆(别名紫海胆,俗称黑刺锅子),最有经济价值。其外形如刺猬,壳内橘瓣似的卵黄是可食部分。属珍贵海产品,营养价值很高,含蛋白质 41%,谷氨酸 6%,做汤卤、做海胆面、煮熟鲜食,味道都很鲜美。做成海胆酱,也为海味酱中的上品。其壳含碳酸钙 90% 以上,煅灰外敷,可解热消炎;少量冲服,可治胃与十二指肠溃疡,并有软坚散结、化痰消肿之功效。

Sea urchins belong to the echinoidea echinodermata with many varieties. Strongylocentrotus nudus (also known as purple sea urchin, commonly known as black thorn pot) from Changdao has the biggest economic value. Its appearance resembles a hedgehog, and the orange petal-like yolk inside is the edible part. It is a precious seafood with high nutritional value. It contains 41% protein and 6% glutamic acid. It tastes delicious when cooked in soup, sea urchin noodles, and cooked fresh food. It can be made into sea urchin sauce, which is also the top grade in sea urchin sauce. Its shell contains more than 90% calcium carbonate. Calcined ash can be used for external application to relieve fever and inflammation. A small amount of it can cure stomach and duodenal ulcers, and has the effects of softening and dispelling swelling, reducing phlegm and swelling.

思考与实践

Thinking and practice

你对上述海珍品还有哪些了解?

怎样对鲜海参进行加工和保存?

参观海参鱼苗场和海参养殖区。

What else do you know about the above sea treasures?

How to process and preserve fresh sea cucumbers?

Visit the sea cucumber fry farm and sea cucumber breeding area.

第二课 带鱼 黑裙 海带 紫菜
Lesson 2 Hairtail, Gymnocorymbus ternetzi, Kelp, Seaweed

带鱼
Hairtail

带鱼又名刀鱼，为暖水性中上层洄游鱼类。其体侧扁，呈带状，一般体长60~120 cm。性凶猛，贪食。主食各种鱼类、毛虾和乌贼等。喜弱光，白天沉到水下层，夜间浮游到表层，有明显的昼夜垂直游移习性。

Hairtail, also known as Ribbonfish, is a mid-pelagic migratory fish in warm water. Its body is flat on the sides, in a ribbon shape, and is generally 60-120 cm long. It is fierce and gluttony. The staple food is various fishes, shrimps and squids.

图 3-2-1 带鱼

It prefers low light, sinks to the underwater layer during the day, and floats to the surface at night, with obvious habit of vertical wandering during day and night.

带鱼在我国各海区均有出产。唯有渤海的带鱼，品种最佳。鱼肉肥嫩细腻，味道鲜美醇香，营养非常丰富。常有销售者特别标明"渤海带鱼"，以推动销售。带鱼鲜食最佳，清蒸、红焖、炒、炸均可，做鲜鱼面味道特香。腌制成咸刀鱼也是民间吃法之一，也可加工成罐头、鱼松或咸干品。其肉鳞、油均可入药，对肝炎和产后乳汁过少有一定疗效。带鱼的表皮银膜还是提炼鱼鳞胶和制造摄影胶卷的工业原料。经化学处理，又可提取一种结晶物质"光磷"，加在塑料和赛璐珞中，可

Often inhabit in the coastal reefs of the islands, or stay deeply between the reefs and caves. Scallops and kelp farms also gather in the sea area. in spring and autumn Every year, there are "passing fish" migrating to the Bohai, inhabiting and foraging in the waters of the Changshan Islands. Fishing mainly depends on angling. There are single-line single hooks or single-line double hooks for single fishing, as well as longline multi-hook (more than one hundred hooks) to put the bottom line to block the fishing. Good anglers catch up with the good tide, find the reef or shipwreck area, one person can catch more than 100 catties in one tide.

长岛海域辽阔,岛礁众多,最适宜黑鱼栖息、觅食和繁殖。一年四季均能捕钓到鲜活黑鱼。"红焖黑鱼"是渔家和饭店最为常见的又较名贵的一道鲜鱼佳肴。

Changdao has a vast sea area and numerous islands and reefs. It is most suitable for snakehead to inhabit, forage and breed. Fresh snakehead can be caught all year round. "Braised snakehead" is the most common and expensive fresh fish delicacy among fishermen and restaurants.

海带
kelp

图 3-2-3 海带

海带,又名昆布、江白菜。原是海底石礁上自然生长的藻类。1958 年从日本引进在我县进行人工栽培试养,获得成功。逐渐发展成为长岛经济支柱产业。长岛海域水深流急,海底礁石密布,出产的海带体长,平直部宽,色泽好,为国内优质品种之一。钦岛乡小浩村生产的海带曾于 1978 年获全国科学大会奖。

Kelp, also known as sea tangle. It was originally the algae that grows naturally on rocky reefs under the sea. In 1958, it was introduced from Japan for artificial cultivation and trial breeding in our county, and succeeded. It was gradually developed into a pillar industry of the Changdao economy. The waters in Changdao are deep and fast, and the seabed reefs are densely covered. The kelp produced is long, wide in the straight part, and good in color. It is one of the domestic high-quality varieties. The kelp produced in Xiaohao Village, Qindao Township, won the National Science Conference Award in 1978.

　　海带经济价值和营养价值都很高，每百克含蛋白质 8.2 克，脂肪 0.1 克，糖 57 克，粗纤维 9.8 克，无机盐 12.9 克，并含有大量的碘、甘露醇和尼克酸等。将海带蒸熟切丝，在炖肉、炒菜、打卤时加入均味美而富营养，也可凉拌菜等。近几年来，一些企业把海带加工成海带丝、海带脯等产品销售，已形成一定的生产规模。在出口创汇方面，海带也发挥了重要作用。海带也是制碘的重要原料，有较高药用价值，可降低胆固醇，防治甲状腺肿大、血管硬化、癞皮病及肝病。从海带中提取的甘露醇，是医治肾功能衰竭、脑炎、急性青光眼等症的急救药。

The economic and nutritional values of kelp are very high. Each 100g of it contains 8.2 grams of protein, 0.1 gram of fat, 57 grams of sugar, 9.8 grams of crude fiber, 12.9 grams of inorganic salt, and a lot of iodine, mannitol and niacin. We can steam the kelp and cut into shreds, add a few of them to the stew, stir-fry, and marinade. making the dishes more delicious and nutritious, and can also be used to make a cold dish. In recent years, some companies have processed kelp into shredded kelp, dried kelp and other products for sale, and have formed a certain scale of production. Kelp has also played an important role in earning foreign exchange through exports. Kelp is also an important raw material for iodine production and has high medicinal value. It can lower cholesterol and prevent goiter, vascular sclerosis, leprosy and liver disease. Mannitol extracted from kelp is an emergency medicine for treating kidney failure, encephalitis, and acute glaucoma.

紫菜
Seaweed

紫菜有圆片形和方片形两种,自然生长在半裸露的礁石上,呈紫褐色或紫红色。全县各岛均有分布,产量少,过去多为群众自采自食,近年已有人工养殖。

紫菜产品多为淡干品,以片薄、表面光滑、紫褐色而有光泽,入口柔软易化,有芳香味为上品。紫菜营养丰富,每百克含蛋白质 24.7 克,脂肪 0.9 克,糖 31.2 克,无机盐 30.3 克,做成汤或包水饺食用,风味独特,味道鲜美,深受人们喜爱。常食可使人皮肤白润细嫩,有一定的美容效果。

图 3-2-4　海紫菜

Seaweed has two types, round slice and square slice. It grows naturally on semi-exposed reefs and shews purple-brown or purple-red. It is distributed all around the islands, and the output is small. In the past, it was mostly collected by the massesand used as their food. In recent years, artificial breeding has been carried out. Seaweed products are mostly light-dried products, and the ones featuring thin slices, smooth surface, being purplebrown and shiny, soft and metting in your mouth, and aromatic taste are regarded as the top grade. Seaweed is rich in nutrients, containing 24.7 grams of protein per 100 grams, 0.9 gram of fat, 31.2 grams of sugar, and 30.3 grams of inorganic salt. It is eaten as soup or dumplings. It has a unique flavor and delicious taste, and it is deeply loved by people. Regular eating of it can allow people's skin to become white and tender, with a certain beauty effect.

思考与实践

Thinking and practice

列举长岛还盛产哪些鱼类和海藻？

Which kind of fish and seaweed are still abundant in Changdao?

第三课　海米 鱼米 海兔酱 海怪酱

Lesson 3　Dried shrimps, Dried fish, sea hare sauce, hermit crab sauce

海米

Dried shrimps

　　海米是鹰爪虾熟晒扒出的虾肉干。因虾体自然弯曲形似鹰爪，以得其名。春秋季捕捞的鲜鹰虾，洗净沥水，倒入烧热的锅中，稍加翻动，虾皮微干，加入 4% 的水，用猛火烧至八成熟，加进 5% 的盐，烧 5 分钟后出锅，晒干后，去皮即成。

图 3-3-1　金钩海米

　　Dried shrimps are just the dried meat pulled of talon shrimps. The shrimp body is naturally curved like an eagle's claw, so it gets the name. Fresh talon shrimps caught in spring and autumn, after being washed and drained, can be poured into a hot pot; and stir-fried slightly, after the prawn skin is slightly dry, add 4% water, burn on a fierce fire until it medium well, add 5% salt, and then cooking for 5 mins, dried, peeled and obtained.

　　判定优质海米，一是虾体弯曲，定是活、鲜虾加工而成，其鲜度高。二是色泽鲜红光亮，系鲜虾在晴天短期晒干。三是品尝或闻之只有鲜美味，无咸、异味，说明盐分合适，没有变质。四是以手握爽利不软为宜，表明干度合适，便于存放。

　　To determine high-quality dried shrimps, one is that the shrimp has a curved body, which must be processed from live and fresh shrimp, and its freshness is high. Secondly, the color is bright red, and the shrimp is dried in the sun for a short period time in sunny days. The third is that the taste or smell is only delicious, no salty or peculiar smell, indicating that the salt is appropriate and there is no deterioration. Fourthly, when being held, it will make you feel sharp, and not soft sharp and not soft, indicating that the dryness is appropriate and easy to store.

鹰虾洄游渤海,途经长岛海域,旺汛时,正值早春和深秋,水凉虾肥,天气干燥凉爽,晒虾干得快,加工出的海米,体肥个大,味道鲜美,所以长岛产的海米,一般是货真质优。

The talon shrimps travels back to the Bohai, passing through the waters of Changdao. It is early spring and late autumn during the prosperous flood season. when the water is cool and the shrimp is fat, and the weather is dry and cool, hence, the shrimp can be dried quickly. The processed dried shrimps are fat, big and taste delicious, so the dried shrimps produced in Changdao are generally genuine and of good quality.

鱼米
Dried fish

鱼米是蒸熟晒成的鲜鱼肉干。大海市季节,新鲜鱼多价廉,岛上人家户户曝晒鱼米,以方便经常食用。剖开鲜鱼肚腹,除去内脏,冲洗干净,切块(小鱼整个)平摆在算子上,稍撒一层精盐,上锅蒸熟,剔除骨刺,将鱼肉弄碎或切成小块,晒干或晾干即成。及时晒干的鱼米,鲜味不减,味道纯正,比鲜鱼另有一番风味,而且极有咬嚼,又容易存放。随时取些温水浸泡,用以烧汤、炒菜、下面、包水饺、蒸菜包均可。

Dried fish is steamed and sun-dried. In the sea market season, fresh fish is very cheaper, and everyone on the island exposes the fish to facilitate regular consumption. Cutting the belly of the fresh fish, removing the internal organs, rinsing, cutting into pieces (the whole small fish) and placing it on the grate, sprinkling a layer of refined salt, and steaming it on the pot, removing the fish bones, and shreding or cutting the fish into small pieces, and then make them dry. The dried fish in time have the undiminished umami and pure taste. It has a different flavor compared with fresh fish, and is extremely chewy and easy to store. Take some warm water to make it soaked at any time and use it for cooking soup, stir-frying, noodles, making dumplings, and steaming vegetables.

现在，有些水产品厂家，批量加工鱼米，装袋销售，很有市场。

Now, some aquatic product manufacturers process the dried fish in batches and sell them in bags, which is very marketable.

海兔酱
Sea Hare Sauce

图 3-3-2　金钩海米

海兔名小乌子，形似梧桐树花，而多叫梧桐花。将新鲜的海兔，反复漂洗干净，加少许精盐拌匀，渍卤几小时，沥去卤水，以兔和盐 1：0.08 的比例，拌盐装罐（或坛）密封。盐多了，不发酵，整兔清汤，吃不出酱味；盐少了，则腐烂变质，不能食用。密封四五天揭盖放"恶气"。再发蒸十多天，烧熟分瓶冷藏，可多次食用。现熥现吃的海兔酱要加盖，防止进蒸馏水而稀汤减味。制好熥熟的海兔酱，酱紫色里透着粉红，成膏状，有特别的鲜香味。蘸有辛辣味的大葱（最佳的是发芽葱），实属上乘的下饭的"就食"。

The sea hare is named Xiaowuzi, which resembles a sycamore tree flower, and is often called a sycamore flower. Rinsing the fresh sea hare repeatedly, adding a little refined salt and mixing well, soaking the brine for a few hours, draining the brine, mixing the salt with the sea hare and the salt at a ratio of 1:0.08, and sealing the jar (or pot). If there is too much salt, it will not be fermented, and the whole sea hare soup will not have the flavor of sauce. If there is less salt, it will become rotten and inedible. Sealing it for four or five days and uncover it to release "bad gas." It will be steamed for another ten days or more, boiled and kept in bottles, and can be eaten many times. The sea hare sauce that is eaten now should be covered to prevent the steamed water from entering the soup and reducing the taste. The sea hare sauce cooked shows purple with pink in it, and is of the shape of a paste with a special fresh fragrance. Dipping with spicy green onions (the best one is sprouted green onions), it is really a good meal.

海兔酱除家庭腌制食用外，已有多家食品厂制成罐头产品，销售全国各地。

In addition to family pickling and consumption, the sea hare sauce has been made canned products by many food factories and sold all over the country.

海怪酱
Hermit crab Sauce

海怪，实名艾氏刺寄生蟹。它有两只钳形大螯，却大小不等；像蟹，却长有肉腹；幼卵生在腹中，长成却附着在外。幼蟹出卵，自找房（空螺壳）住（也称"白住房"）。背着拣来的住房，爬动觅食。逐渐成长，要频频换房。用绳穿螺壳，以"房"诱捕，实属少见"多怪"。

Its Aishi spiny hermit crab. It has two large pincer-shaped claws, but they are of different sizes, like a crab, but with a fleshy belly, the young eggs are born in the abdomen, but they grow to be attached to the outside. When the

图 3-3-3　海怪酱

juvenile crabs come out of their eggs, they will find their own houses (empty snail shells) to live (also called "freely lived houses"). Carrying the picked house, crawling for food. It needs to change rooms frequently with growth. It is really not rare to use a rope to pierce a snail shell and trap it with a "house".

将新鲜海怪，摘去螯腿，粉碎成稠糊状（只用其肉腹制酱，可不粉碎），加一成精盐，搅拌后封于罐内，十天以后即可。

Taking the fresh hermit crab, removing the legs, and crushing it into a thick paste (only using its belly to make sauce, but not crushed), adding 10% of refined salt, and then making them stirred and sealed in the tank, and it will be ready after ten days.

封盖熥熟的海怪酱,呈黄红色,红红的蟹仔,散涌在酱中。味道特别鲜美、香醇,开胃下饭,无以能比。制成的海怪酱罐头,是紧俏热销的海味食品。

The hermit crab that is sealed and heated to be fully well is yellowish-red, and the red crabs are scattered in the sauce. The taste is particularly delicious and mellow, and regarded as an incomparable appetizer. The canned hermit crab sauce is a very popular seafood.

思考与实践

Thinking and practice

根据课文内容试着制作上述特产,并谈谈感受。

According to the content of the text, try to make the above special products and talk about your feelings.

第四课　长岛球石　砣矶砚石
Lesson 4　Long Island Ball Stone, Inkstone

长岛球石
Changdao Ball Stone

在长岛，几乎每座岛屿都产球石，尤以北长山岛月芽湾产的球石最为著名。这些经亿万年海水磨砺而成的球石，大过拳头，小似珍珠，晶莹剔透，珠圆玉润，十分惹人喜爱，是一种天然艺术品。

In Changdao, ball stones are produced almost on every island, especially the ball stones produced in Yueya Bay of North Changshan Island are the most famous. These ball stones, which have been washed by the sea for hundreds of millions of years, are bigger than a fist, small like a pearl, crystal clear, and very cute and regarded as a kind of natural work of art.

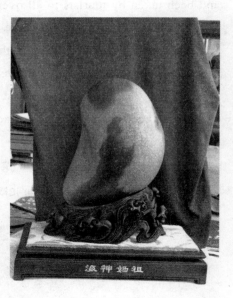

图 3-4-1　长岛球石

宋代文学家苏东坡在《北海十二石记》中赞誉长岛球石"五彩斑斓，秀色粲然"，使长岛球石名闻天下。1979年秋，叶剑英同志游览月芽湾后也赋诗曰："内长山岛月芽湾，勤事渔农并石田，昂价石球生异彩，妇孺岂惜指头艰"。对长岛球石的赞誉也溢于言表。近年来，长岛球石越来越受到人们的喜爱。被游人带到天南海北，世界各地。作为难得的艺术品收藏和欣赏。长岛有不少人，拣其有花纹图案者，置之室中，或展览，或把玩观赏，趣味无穷。如今，长岛美石爱好者已有相当人数，收藏数量颇丰。遴选的精品，参加国内外的美石展评，也屡屡获奖。

Su Dongpo, a writer in Song Dynasty, praised Changdao Ball Stone for its "colorful and beautiful colors" in "The Twelve Stones of the North Sea", which made Changdao Ball Stone famous all over the world. In the autumn of 1979, after visiting Yueya Bay, Comrade Ye Jianying also wrote a poem: "In Changshan Island, Yueya Bay, the fishermen and farmers merged with stone fields, the price of stone balls is splendid, and women and children should not regret that their fingers are difficult." The praise for Changdao Ball Rock is also beyond words. In recent years, Changdao Ball Stone has become more and more popular among people and been taken by tourists to all over the world. It's also regarded as a rare art for collection and appreciation, there are many people in Changdao, who choose those with patterns and put them in the room, or exhibit them, or play and watch them. The fun is endless. Nowadays, there are a considerable number of lovers of beautiful stones on Changdao, and a large number of collections. The selected works have been exhibited at home and abroad, and awarded prizes frequently.

砣矶砚雕
Tuoji Inkstone Carving

图 3-4-2　砣矶砚

砣矶砚雕，过去称砣矶砚，亦称金星雪浪砚，是著名的鲁砚之一。系用砣矶岛特产的金星雪浪石加工而成。此石质地油润细腻，细中有锋，柔中有刚，制成砚，则黑泽如漆，金星闪烁，雪浪腾涌。具有研不起沫，涩不滞笔，油润而不吃墨之特点，受到历代文人墨客的喜爱，许多人视之为宝。

Tuoji Inkstone Carving, formerly called as Tuoji Inkstone, also known as

Jinxing Xuelang Inkstone, is one of the famous Lu Inkstones. It is processed with the Jinxing Xuelang stone, a specialty of Tuoji Island. This stone is oily and delicate in texture, with sharpness shown in the fineness and rigidity in the softness. When made into an inkstone, the black color is like lacquer, shining and surging. It has the following characteristics: no foamed inks ocurred when being ground; being astringent, but without making pen blocked and oily but not making the ink consumed exeremoly. It has been loved by literati in the past and many people regard it as a treasure.

砣矶砚至清代成为贡品，为皇帝和王公大臣们所赏识。上贡给乾隆皇帝的一方砣矶砚，仍保存在故宫博物院内，贡砚为长方形，受墨处宽平，金星雪浪显著，墨池宽广。中刻一蟠（即无角之龙）边刻四螭绕之。砚底刻有乾隆赞誉砣矶砚的绝句："驼基砚刻五螭蟠，受墨何需夸马肝，设以诗中例小品，谓同岛瘦与郊寒"。

Tuoji inkstone became a tribute in the Qing Dynasty and was appreciated by the emperor, princes and ministers. The tribute to Emperor Qianlong is still preserved in the Palace Museum. The tribute inkstone is rectangular, the ink receiving area is wide and flat, the golden star and snow wave are prominent, and the ink pond is wide. In the middle, it is engraved with a curled-up drafon (ie a dragon without horns) and four dragons are engraved around it. The bottom of the inkstone is engraved with quatrain which is praised by Qianlong: "The Tuoji inkstone engraved with five dragons, why do you need to praise horse liver when receiving ink, and set an example in the poem, saying that the same island is thin and the suburbs are cold".

砣矶砚始制于宋朝熙宁年间，兴盛于明、清两朝。至二十世纪三十年代断产。至八十年代，砣矶镇成立工艺美术厂，重新制作砣矶砚，改称为砣矶砚雕。

Tuoji inkstone was firstly made in the Xining period of the Song Dynasty and prospered in the Ming and Qing Dynasties. Its production was ceased in the 1930s. In the 1980s, the arts and crafts factory was established in Tuoji Town to re-produce Tuoji Inkstones and renamed Tuoji Inkstone Sculptures.

思考与实践

Thinking and practice

长岛球石和砣矶砚石各有什么特点？

有条件的同学可以收藏。

What are the characteristics of Changdao Ball Stone and Tuoji Inkstone?

You can collect it.

第四单元　渔家乐

Unit 4　Fisherman' s Holiday Tour

　　长岛渔家乐旅游起始于 1999 年，由南长山镇王沟村首发。至此，长岛从事"渔家乐"旅游项目的渔户 400 多户，床位达 5000 多个。2001 年渔家乐接待游客 20 多万人次，已成为全国知名旅游品牌。渔家乐旅游管理规范，由县政府宏观调控，旅游局行业管理，乡（镇）、村、户三级垂直运作。

　　Fisherman' s Holiday Tour in Changdao started in 1999 and was launched by Wanggou Village, Nanchangshan Town. So far, there have been more than 400 fishermen households engaged in the "Fisherman's Holiday Tour" tourism project on Changdao, with more than 5,000 booths. In 2001, more than 200,000 tourists participated in Fisherman' s Holiday Tour which has become a well-known tourism brand in the country. The management of Fisherman' s Holiday Tour tourism is regulated by the county government's macro-control, and manaped by the tourism bureau industry, and it operates vertically at three levels, township (town), village, and household.

　　渔家乐旅游特色鲜明：食宿在渔家，游乐在海上。

　　Fisherman' s Holiday Tour has distinctive tourism features, accommodation in the fisherman' s house, and pleasure on the sea.

第一课　吃在渔家

Lesson 1　Eating at the Fisherman' s House

渔家乐的饮食极富特色,菜谱以海鲜为主,佐以海产腌制品辅之。主食鲅鱼水饺,手擀鲜鱼面。

The food is rich in characteristics in Fisherman' s Holiday Tour, and the menu is mainly seafood, supplemented by pickled seafood products. The staple food includes mackerel dumplings and hand-made fresh fish noodles.

图 4-1-1　吃在渔家

长岛四面环海,海产品俯首皆是,居民的家常便饭是吃小鱼。同时,螃蟹、爬虾、鹰爪虾、扇贝、贻贝、牡蛎及各种藻类海菜也是桌上常餐。渔家乐饭桌上的鱼、虾、贝、藻等海产都是活鲜,基本上从海里捕捞上来不隔夜就下锅。俗语曰:鲜鱼活虾,少女黄花;臭鱼烂虾,阎王仇家。海产品的鲜与不鲜,营养价值与经济价值都差别很大。渔家烹饪海鲜,以原始加工为主,少雕琢装饰,这样调制出的海鲜原汁原味,鲜度极佳。在价格方面也非常实惠,不像大宾馆、海鲜店那样价格惊人。

Changdao is surrounded by the sea, the seafood is distributed everywhere, and the residents' daily meal is to eat small fish. And crabs, crawling shrimps, talon shrimps, scallops, mussels, oysters and various algae and sea vegetables are also daily meals on the table. The fish, shrimp, shellfish, algae and other seafood on the fisherman' s dinner table are all live and fresh. Basically, they are caught from the sea and cooked on that day. As the saying goes, fresh fish and live shrimps, are more wellcomed, and smelly fish and rotten shrimps will even make the king of Hell feel disgusted. The nutritional value and economic value of seafood are very different. The fisherman's cooking of seafood is mainly based on original processing, so that the seafood prepared in this way has the original flavor and excellent freshness. In terms of price, it is also very affordable, not as expensive as big hotels and seafood shops.

　　游客上午进岛后，由各村委管理人员把游客分请到渔家登记留住。住进渔家已近正午，正好是开午饭的时候。放下沉重的行李，洗一把脸，稍做休息便有渔家大嫂招呼上一顿热气腾腾的渔家饭。满桌子饭菜海鲜占半壁江山，手扒扇贝、贻贝、牡蛎用小盆装盛，每盆都堆起了山头，不由使人联想起海岛人大碗喝酒大块吃肉的豪爽之气。餐桌上的炸小黄花鱼，焖黑鱼，凉拌海蜇皮、裙带菜等家常小吃也毫不逊色，满

图 4-1-2　吃在渔家

桌子海鲜五彩斑斓，鲜香四溢，叫人垂涎欲滴。渔家乐菜谱设置极为科学，除海鲜之外，还配有几样蔬菜及汤，目的是营养搭配更趋合理，同时也是为照顾各地旅客的不同口味。千万不要小瞧这些青菜，它们可全是渔家自种的绿色食品。

　　After the tourists entered the island in the morning, the management staff of the village committee sent the tourists to the fishermen's house to register. It was almost noon when moving into the fisherman's house, it happened to be lunch. Putting down the heavy luggage, washing face, and taking a break, the fisherman greeted a steaming fisherman's meal. The table was full of food and seafood, and the hand-chopped scallops, mussels, and oysters which were served in small pots. Each pot was piled up like hills, which reminded people of the boldness of people from the islands who drank large bowls of wine and ate large pieces of meat. The fried small yellow croaker, braised black fish, cold jellyfish, wakame and other homemade snacks on the table were also no less wonderful. The colorful seafood on the table was colorful, fresh and delicious, and it was mouth-watering. The fisherman' s menu is extremely scientific. In addition to seafood, it also comes with a few vegetables and soups. The purpose is to make the nutritional mix more reasonable and to cater for the different tastes of tourists from all over the world. Don't underestimate these vegetables, they are all green food grown by fishermen.

热情好客的渔家大嫂前后忙乎,不停巡视,看哪桌子的菜吃空了,不断添加,就怕游客吃不饱。有的旅客吃起海鲜胃口大开,添加几次还欲壑难填,嫂子也毫不吝惜,只要有存货,便大盘盛上,让游客过一次海鲜瘾。

The hospitable fisherman was busy around and kept walking around the table, seeing whether the dishes were emptied or not, and constantly adding them, fearing that the tourists would not be full. Some tourists had a great appetite for seafood, and it was hard to fill it up after adding a few times. The fisherman was also not stingy. As long as there was stock, it will be served, allowing tourists to enjoy themselves to the full .

晚餐以中午的菜谱为班底,主食一般是手擀鲜鱼面。渔家乐晚饭最大特色是游客可以走进厨房参与其中。如果想吃长岛名贵的海鲜,像鲍鱼、海参、海胆、港湾贝等,可以自己掏腰包购买,由渔家乐免费加工,保你吃上一顿物美价廉的海珍品。游客还可以把在海上游玩时的收获,像垂钓的鱼,捡拾的绵蝛(锈凹螺)、香蝛(绵蝛螺)带回渔家,品尝自己的劳动果实。吃晚饭时,可把饭桌移到渔家大院或乡间路旁的绿荫底下,边欣赏渔村小景,边品味海鲜,真可谓美味可食,秀色可餐;靠近海边的渔家乐,索性把饭桌移至海边,在散发着阵阵海腥味的海潮拍打声中,在闪耀着五颜六色的大海晚霞中,把酒临风,笑谈餐饮。

Dinner is based on the lunch menu, and the staple food is usually hand-rolled fresh fish noodles. The biggest feature of the fisherman' s dinner is that visitors can enter into the kitchen to participate. If you want to eat the precious seafood of Changdao, such as abalone, sea cucumber, sea urchin, harbour scallops, etc., you can buy it at your own pocket, and the fisherman will process it for free, so that you can eat a meal of high-quality and inexpensive seafood. Visitors can also bring back the harvests from fishing in the sea, such as fishing fish, pickled snails, to the fisherman's home to taste the fruits of their labor. When having dinner, you can move the dining table to the fisherman' s courtyard or under the green shade on the side of the country road, enjoying the small scenery of the fishing village while savoring seafood. It is really delicious. As for the fisher' s house near the sea people there simply move the dining table on the seaside. In the sound of the sea tide that exudes the smell of the sea, and in the shining colorful sunset refleated in the sea, they bring the wine to the wind and talk about catering.

　　第二天刚刚露出晨曦，渔家大嫂便起身忙乎一顿可口的渔家小吃。小菜有咸鱼、鱼酱、海兔酱、虾酱，种类繁多；海带丝有辣的、甜的，五花八门，还有香椿，韭菜花……这些小菜不油不腻，清爽可口，个个都是下饭的菜。饭食是渔家炕锅蒸的大馒头、玉米饼子。大馒头个头足有半斤来重，全是手工锼出来的，蒸出来的馒头即暄腾又有筋道，吃起来香喷喷，真是名副其实的香饽饽。玉米饼子有手巴掌大小，个个金灿灿的。这些饼子大都是玉米面和黄豆面配制而成，营养极为丰富。长岛俗语有"喇喇肠子"之说，意思是说要常吃粗食，这样饮食对身体健康大有益处。如果赶上农收季节，游客还能吃上金灿灿的、鲜嫩嫩的煮玉米，吃起来真的比城里好吃，这可是刚从地里掰来的，还带着泥土的清香。渔家的稀饭花样颇多，早饭一般做玉米面粥，黄米粥，大米粥。最有特色的是玉米馇子粥，渔家农收时把玉米磨成碎粒儿，做早饭时放在炕锅里熬制，燃料全用干草或木材下脚料，这样熬制的玉米馇子粥味道纯正、黏稠，玉米粒儿像散珠碎玉，金光闪闪，吃起来香喷喷，甜滋滋，有咬头。

　　The next day, just after the dawn, the wife of the fisherman got up and was busy with a delicious fisherman's snack. The side dishes included salted fish, fish sauce, sea hare sauce, and shrimp sauce, varied in kinds; the kelp shreds were spicy, sweet, etc., as well as toon and chives...,which were not greasy, but more refreshing and delicious. It was dish appropriate for dinner. The meals were big buns and corn cakes steamed in the fisherman's pot in kang (a heatable brick bed. The big steamed buns weighed half jinca unit of weight, $=\frac{1}{2}$ kilogram) and they were all made by hand. The steamed buns were both tender and chewy, and tasted delicious. It was a veritable sweet and glutinous rice cake. The corn tortillas were palm-sized, all golden. Most of these pancakes were made of corn flour and soybean flour, which were extremely nutritious. There was a saying in Changdao, "La la intestines", which meant that you should eat coarse food frequently. This diet was very beneficial to your health. If it catched up with the harvest season, visitors can still eat golden, tender and boiled corn. It tasted better than in the city. It was freshly picked from the ground and had the fragrance of the earth. There were many kinds of porridge in fishermen's family. For breakfast, cornmeal porridge, yellow rice porridge and rice porridge were usually made. The most distinctive feature was the corn porridge. The corn porridge was made by grinding corn into morsels when harvesting, and boiled in a kang pot for breakfast. the hay or wood scraps were used as fuel. This corn porridge was cooked. It tasted pure and sticky. The corn kernels were like scattered beads and jade, with golden light. It tastes delicious and sweet.

渔家的特色小吃，堪称一绝。如果在渔家住的时间略长一些（一般2天），渔家大嫂会为游客包上一顿鲅鱼水饺或海蛎子水饺等。鲅鱼水饺这可是长岛名吃，吃起来会让人流连忘返。渔家乐包的鲅鱼水饺个头大，每个足足有2～3两重，像蒸包大小。包鲅鱼水饺极为讲究，从拌馅、擀皮、煮法到吃饺子用的调料，工序繁多、独到。因此煮出来的饺子清齐，爽滑，干挺，闪亮。吃时佐芥末调料，口味重不腻，通体鲜爽。在渔家乐吃鲅鱼水饺，一般人都会超过平时的食量。渔家乐的鲅鱼水饺称得上饺子中的极品，苏东坡曰：日啖荔枝三百颗，不辞长作岭南人。吃过长岛鲅鱼水饺，恐怕这种感觉不禁油然而生。

The fisher's specialty snacks are very special. If you stay at the fisher's house longer (usually 2 days), the fisher's wife will make a meal of mackerel dumplings or sea oyster dumplings for tourists. Mackerel dumplings are famous on Changdao, and they will make you miss it. The mackerel dumplings in Fisherman's Holiday Tour are big, each with 100 to 150 grams, just like a steamed bun. Mackerel dumplings are very particular, from mixing stuffing, rolling the skin, cooking methods to the seasonings for eating dumplings, the process is numerous and unique. Therefore, the cooked dumplings are clean, smooth, dry and shiny. When eating with mustard seasoning, the taste is heavy and not greasy, and the whole body is fresh and refreshing. Most people will eat more than usual in Fisherman's

Holiday Tour. The mackerel dumplings of Fisherman's Holiday Tour can be called the best among dumplings. Su Dongpo said: If I eat 300 lychees every day, I am willing to live in Lingnan forever. I've eaten mackerel dumplings in Changdao, and the feeling is just like what Dongpo have said.

第二课　住在渔家

Lesson 2　Living in a Fisherman's House

长岛拔地崛起于黄、渤海之交,峰光波影,云笼霞帔,变幻无穷,景色十分秀丽。住在大海里的小渔村,会给人一种超拔出世的感觉,既幽深静谧,又海阔天空。到岸请君四周望,渔家乐就在海中央。

Changdao rises up at the turn of the Yellow Sea and the Bohai

图 4-2-1　吃在渔家

sea, with peaks and shadows, clouds, with endless changes and beautiful scenery. Living in a small fishing village in the sea will give people a sense of super-worldliness, and being deep and quiet, and vast. When you get to the shore, please look around. The fisherman's family is in the middle of the sea.

长岛渔民人均住房面积达 24 ㎡,被确定为渔家乐的住房面积更是宽绰有余,建筑面积达 80~100 ㎡,二层别墅小楼开渔家乐的,面积多达 200 ㎡以上。通长一户渔家乐住游客 8~10 人,每个房间住 2~4 人。在安排住宿时,先征求游客的意见后再作安排。凡家庭旅游的,一般把一家人安排在一个房间;单位集体旅游的,朋友之间搭好伙后一般也安排在同一个房间。

The per capita housing area of Changdao fishermen is 24 square meters, and the housing area that is determined to be used for very a Fisherman's Holiday Tour is more than adequate, with a construction area of 80-100 square meters. The two-story villa building for Fisherman's Holiday Tour covers an area of more than 200 square meters. Usually, 8 to 10 tourists can accommodate in Fisherman's Holiday

Tour, and 2 to 4 people in each room. When arranging accommodation, firstly ask the opinions of tourists. For family travel, usually arranged in the same room. For unit travel, friends are usually arranged in the same room after organizing group.

　　海岛民风淳朴，人情厚道，住在渔家就像在家。在渔家乐，没有类似旅店的时刻表，你可夜里闲逛，不管多晚总有人为你开门；在房间里你可彻夜娱乐，不会有斥责声，有的只是渔家大嫂和蔼的劝告声"早点休息"。当你遇到麻烦需要帮助时，渔家大嫂就像一位家人呵护在你身旁问长问短；当你想要了解海岛的风土人情，渔家大嫂又像一位相识多年的老朋友一样跟你拉家常；当你要出海游玩时，大嫂会挨个询问"太阳帽带了？手套拿了没有？"。住在渔家，虽没有星级宾馆的豪华，但这里多的是人间真情——温馨，尊重，关爱，沟通。许多游客与渔家结下深厚的友谊，他们互留地址，互通音信，为的是来日方长。

The people on the island are honest and kindly, and living in a fisher's house is like being at home. In Fisherman's Holiday Tour, there was no timetable. You can hang out at night, no matter how late it was, someone will always open the door for you. In the room, you can entertain all night without being scolded, and some were just the kindly advice from the fisherman's wife, such as rest early. When you were in trouble and needed help, the fisherman's wife was like a family member who was beside you to ask questions. When you wanted to understand the customs of the island, the fisherman's wife who will follow you was just like an old friend who had known each other for many years. When you were going to play at sea, fisherman's wife will ask one by one, "Did you wear a sun hat? Did you take your gloves?". Living in fisher's house, although it did not have the luxury of a star-rated hotel, there were many true feelings here-warmth, respect, care, and communication. Many tourists and fishermen had forged a deep friendship. They exchanged addresses and messages in order to stay in touch for a long time.

　　渔家乐住宿设施齐全。申请开渔家乐渔户必须经过村委会严格检查验收，渔户必须配备统一的木床（个别也有用席梦思床），统一的褥垫，统一的床单，统一的巾被。夏天每张床都要挂上蚊帐，铺上竹制凉席。走进渔家乐卧室，整个房间清洁、整齐、敞亮、温馨。在渔家乐耳房、平房顶上都装有太阳能洗澡设备，洗浴在平房或耳房里，房间一般为 8~10 ㎡，可供 4~5 人同时洗浴。

The fisherman's accommodation facilities are complete. Fishermen who applied to open a fisherman's house must undergo strict inspection and acceptance by the village committee. The fishermen must be equipped with a unified wooden bed (sometimes also use Simmons beds), a unified mattress, a unified bed sheet, and a unified quilt. In summer, the mosquito nets must be hung on bed and covered with bamboo mats. Walking into the bedroom of Fisherman's Holiday Tour, the whole room was clean, tidy, bright and warm. The penthouse and bungalows of Fisherman's Holiday Tour were equipped with solar-powered bathing equipment. The bathing was allowed in the bungalow or penthouse. The room was generally 8~10 square meters, which can accommodate 4~5 people at the same time.

住在渔家十分悠闲。清晨,你可起个早朝,在渔家后院侍弄菜地里的蔬菜,浇灌院子里的花朵,喂喂鸡,逗逗狗,帮帮炊。你也可沿着乡间的小路跑步晨练,呼吸呼吸海岛清晨沁人心脾的空气,跑到山顶满眼绿色,山桃槐花争妍斗艳,清香扑鼻,随手采撷几朵戴在姑娘头上,就是一位乡村小芳。登高眺望,渔家乐红瓦绿树,炊烟袅袅,一幅乡间水彩画尽收眼底。傍晚,在渔家大门口,渔家大秧歌闪亮登场,有过海的八仙、飞天的牛郎织女、西游的孙猴子猪八戒,后面跟着一群蟹兵虾将和众多的美丽贝壳。扭秧歌的个个神采飞扬,挥舞着扇子、彩段、龙头杖、长烟袋,或者禅杖、朴刀,真是五颜六色,五花八门,在村口围成一大圈,待那唢呐钹镲皮鼓铜锣响起,便扭起来,跳起来,逗起来,或急或缓,

图 4-2-2　渔家过大年

或分或合,渲染出一派祥和、红火的欢乐气氛。渔村人像过节一样,百十户人家齐出动,把村街挤得水泄不通。看呀,喊呀,笑呀,个个乐弯了腰。渔家自己组织的秧歌队,不分年关节日,只要大家想看,就随时拉出来,扭一场,跳一场,逗一场,乐一场。夜晚,明月当空,海风拂面,在渔家院子里坐着渔家马扎子,谈天说地,传说海的故事,那份轻松休闲,真不亚于城里的夜总会。夜深了,渔村睡了,睡在大海那温馨的臂弯里,人们就连夜里也做着海的梦。

Living in the fisher's house was very leisurely. In the early morning, you can get up early in the morning and serv the vegetables in the backyard of the fisherman's house, water the flowers in the yard, feed the chickens, tease the dogs, and help with the cooking. You can also run morning exercises along the country roads, breath in the refreshing air of the island early in the morning, and run to the top of the mountain for glutting their eyes; when picking eyes, the peach and acacia flowers were beautiful and fragrant, when picking a few flowers and wearing them on the girl's head, can make the girl more beautiful is presented. Climbing up and looking down, Fisherman' s Holiday Tour had red tiles and green trees, smoke curling up, and a watercolor painting of the countryside is presented with a panoramic view. In the evening, at the gate of the fisherman's house, the fisherman's Yangko made its debut. There were the Eight Immortals who crossed the sea, the flying Niulang and the Weaver Girl, and the Monkey King and Pig Bajie who traveled to the west, followed by a group of crabs soldiers, shrimp generals and many beautiful shells. All the people who twisted the Yangko were flying, waving fans, color segments, dragon head sticks, long pipes, or Zen sticks and simple swords. They were really colorful and varied. They formed a big circle at the entrance of the village. When the suona horn, cymbal drum and gong sounded, then they twisted up, jumped up, teased, hurriedly or slowly, divided or combined, rendering a peaceful and prosperous joyous atmosphere. The people in the fishing village were like celebrating a festival, and hundreds of households moved out, crowded the village streets. They looked, shouted, laughed, and bent over for joy. The Yangko team was organized by fisherman's family, regardless of year and day, as long as everyone wanted to watch, they can gather to play at any time, twist, jump, make fun, and have fun. At night, with the bright moon in the sky and the sea breeze blowing, sitting in the fisherman' s yard, the fisherman's Ma Zhazi, a folding stool chatting and telling the story of the sea, making you feal no less relaxing than a nightclub in the city. Late at night, the fishing village slept in the warm arms of the sea, and people dreamed of the sea even at night.

第三课　游在海上
Lesson 3　Travelling in the sea

　　长岛美景如画,景点众多,可游玩的地方实在太多。但最具海岛特色的游玩,当推渔家乐开辟的随船海上游项目。俗语说"不到长城非好汉",同样,进岛不到海上游等于白忙乎,只有深入大海,才能了解海岛风土人情,才能领略大海秀美风光。

　　Changdao has picturesque scenery and numerous attractions, and there were so many places to visit. However, the most island-style play was the marine traveling project developed by Fisherman' s Holiday Tour. As the saying goes, "If you don't reach the Great Wall, you' re not a hero." Similarly, you can' t get into the real island until you reach the sea. Only by going deep sea can you understand the island' s customs and enjoy the beautiful scenery of the sea.

　　近海作业游。一般情况下,游客在船老大带领下,乘坐渔家的"195"船只(12马力,坐10人)或者乘坐"挂尾机"船只(俗称水上摩托,8.5马力,坐8人)出海作业,渔船开至离海岸1千米以内的海区里,项目主要是拔蟹笼,扒海虹,放针良船等。蟹笼制作不十分复杂但很科学,取直径4～6毫米的钢筋,圈3个直径为40～60厘米的圆圈,再用1米左右长同规格的钢筋3根,将三个圈连成筒状,然后用废网衣全面包缝起来,只在上、中、下层分别留3～5个诱蟹洞。洞口也用旧网衣缝成筒状,外口10厘米左右,用铁丝撑圆,筒路渐窄,蟹子只能进不能出。游客可将网筒(内放有诱饵),沉于海底与海底平。螃蟹嗅觉甚灵,闻味迅速聚来。水清、浅处可视来蟹多少,及时提网捉蟹;水深混浊时,可10分钟左右提网筒看一次,时间长了,饵易被蟹吃光。当然,游客都是捉蟹新手,难免手忙脚乱,这不打紧,站在船头露出光光的脊背和黛黑臂膀的船老大就在你左右,经过他的指点你就会成为行家里手。此法捉蟹既有情趣,笼笼又有真家伙,其乐无穷,回去吃一顿螃蟹大餐毫无问题。扒海虹可是个苦活,船老大喊着渔家号子,众人一齐把海中的海虹架子拔出海面挂在船帮上,海虹通体墨黑,个体肥大,在阳光的照耀下,像颗颗黑珍珠。要扒下这些海虹并非易事,因为海虹粘在架子上,非要花些功夫才能扒下,难怪游客回到渔家吃上自己亲

图 4-2-2　渔家过大年

自扒下的海虹时,会发出“谁知盘中餐,粒粒皆辛苦”的感叹。最有情致的是在海中放针良船。所谓放针良船,就是放钓针良鱼的船。这个“船”是象征性的,只用 5 cm 宽、50 cm 左右长的木板 2 块、25 cm 长的一块,钉制一个平面三角木架,中间再嵌一横木,装上一支拇指粗、40 cm 高的竹竿,名曰桅杆,桅杆上挂 2 尺布为帆,这便是沿线钓针良鱼的船。在海中,悠坐船头,手扯长线,借风放船,以船带线,沿线挂钩垂钓针良鱼。小船飘飘悠悠,宛如放网筝,不亲临其境,你很难体会到它那妙不可言的情趣。乐滋滋地放出去,充满着满腔希望,笑嘻嘻地收回来,收获丰硕的果实,可谓放长线,钓鱼多。有幸者,如遇上针良鱼群,沿丝挂满了鱼,鱼体洁白如银,酷似一串银棱,在阳光下璨璨生辉,十分壮观。孤岛探幽游。长岛大小岛屿 32 个,其中 20 多个为无居民岛。为适应游客猎奇、探险、刺激的心理,渔家乐最新推出了孤岛探幽游项目,就是把游客送到无居民岛上,锻炼游客的生存能力。目前,选定的岛屿为小竹山岛。小竹山岛,面积为 0.24 km²,岛岸线长 2 km,最高海拔 97.2 m,距县城航海时间为 2 小时左右。岛内无淡水,少树木,多峭壁,但海岸线海产多。孤岛探幽游项目人选一般为 20～50 人之间,游客彼此熟悉,身体健康,能互相帮助、关心。探险时间安排在上午 9 点钟左右由渔家乐派船(100 马力以上)送至小竹山岛,下午 4 点钟左右接回渔家乐。要参加这个项目,游客必须提前做好一切准备工作,备足淡水,带好炊具,拿着急救药物等等。当然,不少游客刻意少带东西,为的是练练自己的生存能力。

Offshore operation tour. On normal circumstances, under the leadership of the boss of the boat, tourists took the fisherman's “195” boat (12 horsepower, seated 10 people) or a “tail-mounted” boat (commonly known as water scooter,

8.5 horsepower, 8 people) to go to sea for work, and the fishing boat was driven in the sea area within 1 kilometer from the coast, the main items were crab cages, mussels, and needle boats. The fabrication of crab cages was not very complicated but scientific. Taking steel bars with a diameter of 4-6 mm, making 3 circles with a diameter of 40-60 cm, and then use 3 steel bars of the same specification about 1 meter long for each to connect the three circles. The tube was then fully covered with a waste net, leaving only 3-5 crab traps in the upper, middle, and lower layers. The opening of the hole was also sewn into a tube shape with old nets, the outer opening was about 10 cm, and the round was supported by iron wire. The tube path became narrower, and crabs can only enter but not exit. Visitors can sink the net tube (with bait inside) and sink it on the bottom of the sea. Crabs have a very good sense of smell, and will gather quickly by smelling. When the water was clear and shallow, you can see how many crabs come in. Picking up the net to catch the crabs in time. When the water was deep and muddy, you can lift the net tube once every 10 minutes. After a long time, the bait was easy to be eaten by the crabs. Of course, tourists were all novices in crab catching, and it was inevitable that they were in a hurry. The boss with the bare back of the bow and arms was at your side. After his guidance, you will become an expert. This method of catching crabs is so funny, and there were real crabs in the cage, and it was full of fun. There was no problem going back to eat a crab meal. Picking up the mussels was a hard job. The old boat yelled the fisherman's songs. Everyone pulled out the mussels shelf out of the sea and hung it on the boat gang. The mussels was black in its entirety, and the individual was fat. Under the sun, it looked like black pearls. It was not easy to pick off these mussels, because they sticked to the shelf, and it took some effort to pick them off. No wonder tourists returned to the fisher's house to eat the mussels that they had personally grabbed, and will say every grain comes from hard and laborious toil. The most affectionate thing was to set the needle boat in the sea. The so-called good needle boat was a boat for good needle fishing. This "boat" is symbolic. Using only 2 wooden 5 cm wide and about 50 cm long boards, and one 25 cm long boards, nailed to form a flat triangular wooden frame, with a horizontal wood embedded in the middle, equipped with a thumb thick, 40-centimeter-high bamboo pole, called a mast, and a 2-foot cloth was hung on the mast as a sail. This was the boat for long-line fishing. In the sea, sitting on the bow of the boat, pulling the long line with your hands, releasing the boat by the wind, using the boat to bring the line, and the extension line to hook the needle fish. The boat floating around was like flying a kite. If you didn't visit it in person, it was hard for you to appreciate its indescribable taste. It was released happily, full of hope, and returned with a grin, enabling a lot of fruit harvested. It may be called played a much longer game. Fortunately, if you encountered a school of needle fish, it will be hung along the silk. The body of the fish which was as white as silver was just like a string of silver ribs, shining brilliantly in the sun, which was very spectacular. Exploring the lonely island tour. There are 32 large and small islands on Changdao, of which more than 20 are non-inhabited islands. In order to adapt to tourists' psychology of curiosity, adventure, and excitement, Fisherman' s Holiday Tour recently launched the isolated island exploring tour project, which is to send tourists to non-inhabited islands to exercise their survival ability. Currently, the selected island is Xiaozhushan island which has an area of 0.24 square kilometers, a coastline of 2 kilometer, and a maximum altitude of 97.2 meters. It takes about 2 hours to sail from this place to county. The island features no fresh water, few trees, and many cliffs, but the coastline is rich in seafood. The candidates for the isolated island exploration tour project are generally between 20-50 people. The tourists are familiar with each other, in good health, and can help and care for each other. The expedition is scheduled at around 9 o'clock in the morning, and tourists are to be sent to Xiaozhushan Island by a fisherman ship (above 100 horsepower), and taken back to fishermen's family around 4 o'clock in the afternoon. To participate in this project, visitors must make all preparations in advance, prepare enough fresh water, bring cooking utensils, take first aid medicine and so on. Of course, many tourists deliberately bring less things in order to exercize their survivability.

海边篝火晚会。夕阳西下,忙碌了一天的游客可事先与当地渔户商定择一平坦岸滩,点燃一堆篝火,即兴进行一场晚会。平整洁白的沙滩、浩瀚无垠的大海,熊熊燃烧的篝火,热情豪放的人群,此情此景你可尽情的唱,尽情地跳……,卡拉 OK,清唱,每首都精彩;交谊舞、水兵舞、渔家大秧歌每曲都火热。海边的篝火晚会,粗犷、热烈、率直、浪漫,简直就是一曲不经修饰和美化的野性歌谣。晚会的高潮是燃放烟火,刹那间耀眼的光亮映红了天空,照亮了大海,人们在海边忘情地欢呼,嬉戏,拥抱大海的洗礼。

Bonfire at the sea. As the sun sets, tourists who have been busy for a day can negotiate with local fishermen in advance to choose a flat beach, light a bonfire, and have an impromptu party. The flat and clean white beach, the vast sea, the burning bonfire, and the enthusiastic crowd, in this situation, you can sing and dance to your heart's content... Karaoke, singing without accompaniment, every song is wonderful, ballroom dance, sailor dance, and fishmen's Yangko each of them is enthusiastic. The bonfire party by the sea is rough, warm, frank, and romantic. It is simply a wild ballad without modification and beautification. The climax of the party was the display of fireworks. The dazzling light reflected the sky and illuminated the sea. People cheered, laughed, and embraced the sea.

第四课　渔家过大年
Lesson 4　The Fisherman Celebrates the New Year

过惯了城里的年,不妨到渔家体验过年的滋味。海岛人世代与海为伴,吃海产、住海屋、听海风、乘海浪,养成了海的性格、海的气质和海的风韵。喝酒要海碗,说话亮海口,办起事情来,也有海的呼啸、海的汹涌。海岛渔家的这些清晰的海洋文化烙印,在世世代代的潜移默化中,一直沿袭至今。越是民俗

图 4-4-1　渔家过大年

的越是人类共同的财富,到渔家过大年不仅仅是过节,更是品味海岛民俗文化。

Once you are used to the New Year in the city, you might as well go to the fisherman's house to experience the taste of Chinese New Year. People on the islands have been with the sea for generations, eating seafood, living in a sea house, listening to the sea breeze, and riding the waves. They have cultivated the character, temperament and charm of the sea. Drinking by large bowl, talking by large mouth, and getting things done, as if the roar and the surging of sea. These clear maritime cultural imprints of the island fishermen have been carried on to this day which exert subtle influence on generations. Folklore is just the common wealth of mankind. To spend the New Year at a fisherman is not only a festival, but also a taste of the island's folk culture.

春节时分,正是渔闲季节,也是一家老少团圆的节日。海上捕捞,讲究的是鱼汛,鱼汛来临渔民有时几个月都回不了家。而到了春节,渔民带着丰收的喜悦

与家人团圆,这个时候才是一家
人最喜庆的时刻,整个村子也沉浸
在欢乐之中。春节前夕,人们习惯
要忙年,过年的乐趣也就在一个
"忙"字上。渔家忙年很有文化,游
客若在渔家过大年,就能体验到这
风风火火忙年的喜庆。

图 4-4-2　渔家过大年

The Spring Festival is the
fishing and leisure season, and it is
also a festival for the reunion of the young and the old. Fishing at sea is concerned
with fish floods, and fishermen sometimes cannot return home for several months
when the fish floods come. In the Spring Festival, fishermen reunite with their
families with the joy of harvest. This was the most happiest time for the family,
and the whole village was also immersed in joy. On the eve of the Spring Festival,
people were accustomed to busy New Year, the fun of the New Year also lied in the
word "busy". The fisherman's busy year had deep culture. If you spent the New
Year at the fisherman, you can experience the joy of this busy year.

在海岛,时到农历腊月初八,即陆续办置年货。昔日,尽管各家贫富不一,但
都要把平日攒积的留着过年,意思不明,都上一个新台阶。

On the islands, it was the eighth day of the twelfth lunar month, that was,
to buy new year goods one after another. In the old days, despite the differences
between the rich and the poor, each family had to save what they had accumulated
for the New Year, and each family's life and their own experience had taken them
to a new level.

腊月二十前后,家家户户都要打扫灰。一年有 360 天,凡是平日扫帚没到的
地方,都要"推陈、出新"。这天,家庭的主妇是组织者,男人们多用长杆绑一笤
帚,从高处的屋笆到低处的桌底、柜后,像除妖魔一样,认真彻底地把尘埃扫干
净。而后垫地、掏灰、清理烟道、刷墙;主妇则糊炕缝、擦门窗。炕上要铺新草、新
席,大凡该换的则换,该补的则补。清净、更新是宗旨,谁也别图省事,糊弄人。

Around the twentyth of the twelfth lunar month, every household must clean up the ashes. Wherever the broomsticks do not reach on weekdays during 360 days a year, we must make it cleaned, which stands for renovating the old and bringing forth the new. On this day, the housewife of the family was the organizer. The men used long poles to tie a broom. From the rasfing of house to the bottom of the table and the cabinet, they swept the dust away, like dispelling of demons. Then, ground treatment, ash removal, cleaning of flue and painting of wall are carried out; the housewife pasted the kang seams, wiped the doors and windows. New grass and new mats should be laid on the kang, replaced, and supplemented. Purity and renewal are the purpose, and everyone should make all efforts.

渔家过年要忙活的事太多，头年的十几天都是倒计时的。尤其女主人，拆洗衣被，擦拭家什，还要蒸、炸、包、炒各种年食，忙得加夜班；男人们则挑水、劈柴，打扫环境卫生，办置年货……可谓全家老小都有分工，大人孩子都在盼年、忙年的气氛中迎年。

There were too many things for the fisherman to work on during the New Year. More than ten days before the new year were countdown. Especially the hostess, unpacking the laundry, cleaning the household items, cooking all kinds of New Year's food by steaming, frying, etc. busy working overtime. The men carried water, chopped materials, cleaned the environment, and bought new year goods... all the families have done their own work. And both adults and children welcome the new year in an atmosphere of anticipation and busy working.

辞了灶，年来到。腊月二十三日，亦叫过小年。这天，锅台后要请新灶王爷。新请的灶王爷对联是：上天言好事，下界保平安。横批是：一家之主。腊月二十五日，是蒸饽饽的日子。渔家大海盆里发几十斤面，摊在面板上，要调得硬，揉得匀，饽饽才能蒸得圆整、起浮，有筋道。更重要的做供品，马虎不得，有的面不开，或碱少了发酸，或火候不到，宁肯另做，上供桌的饽饽面坯足有一斤重。同时，随着蒸饽饽还要做一些猪头、羊头、圣虫、元宝等面食。这些兽食，身插红枣，口衔硬币，旨在早日发财，发洋财，财源不尽。

When bidding farewell to be kitchen god, the new year will come. The 23rd day of the twelfth lunar month is also called small year. On this day, behind the pot, please invite the kitchen god. The newly-invited couplet for this invitation is. The heavens say good things, and the lower realms keep safe. The horizontal scroil is: the head of the family. The twenty-fifth day of the twelfth lunar month is a day of steaming bun. The dozens of jin of doughs were leavened and spread on the panel. They must be hardened and kneaded evenly, so that the pastry will be steamed to be round, floating, and chewy. It is more important to make articles of tribute. Some doughs do not be well leavened, or the alkali is less becoming, sour, or the fire is not enough. I would rather make another tribute. The pasta on the table weighs one jin. At the same time, along with the steamed pasta, some flour-made food such as pig's head, sheep's head, sacred insects, ingots, etc. are also to be made. These beast shaped foods, with red dates in their bodies and coins in their mouths, stand for making money as soon as possible and make foreign wealth, with inexhaustible sources of wealth.

腊月二十六日至二十九日，炸鱼、熬碗、蒸糕、包粽子、包"隔年陈"包子（准备正月吃，意在从今年吃到明年，视为富有）。二十八或二十九日，封对子、挂家谱，并到船上挂旗。水缸要添满，不能留一点空缺，象征事事圆圆满满。

From the twenty-sixth to twenty-ninth of the twelfth lunar month, fried fish, boiled bowls, steamed cakes, wrapped zongzi, and wrapped "the next year old" steamed buns for the new year (prepared to eat in the first month of new year, meaning making it to be eaten from this year to next year, regarded as wealth). On the 28th or 29th, sealing the pair, hanging the family tree and flag on the ship. The water tank must be filled up, and no vacanay should be left. It is a sign of success.

大年三十下午，各户的男主人要率领儿孙们，到自家的祖坟地请先辈们来家过年，俗称"请神"。"神"请回家后，不扫地，不泼水，不说粗话、脏话，清一色的吉利话。入夜，全家老小守岁，品味各类糖果，谈论一年的收成。除夕夜一过，全村鞭炮齐鸣，渔家人特别器重鞭炮，因为它集红火、光亮、响当于一身，这脆脆的鞭炮声倾注了渔家人对美好生活的憧憬，在渔家过年别的可不买，鞭炮不可不买。未等天亮，村中人群往来，先到本家长者拜年，再去亲邻各户，全村家家都要走遍，人人都要问好。

On the 30th afternoon of the Lunar New Year, the male owner of each household will lead his children and grandchildren to the ancestral cemetery of his family and invite the ancestors to come to celebrate the New Year called "invitation of God". When the God was invited to home, do not sweep the floor, splash water, speak foul language, or say swear words and only the auspicious words can wack around. At night, the whole family waited the new year, tasted all kinds of sweets, and talked about the year's harvest. After New Year's Eve, the whole village set off firecrackers. The fishermen especially valued firecrackers because they stood for prosperity, brightess and loudness. The crisp sound of firecrackers manifested the fisherman vision for a better life. Among others, the firecracker is most necessany one to celebrate Spring Festival for fishermen firecrackers. Before dawn, the people in the village came and went to visit their parents first, and then to the neighbors and families. The whole village had to be visited, and everyone had to say hello.

正月初一渔家吃的饺子里包有"彩头"。吃到硬币，象征发财，糖代表甜蜜，糕代表节节高。表现了渔家图吉祥、向往富有的意愿。吃完饺子，人们都涌向街头，街头人山人海观看耍龙、渔家大秧歌。

On the first day of the first lunar month, the fisherman's dumplings were made with "good luck". Eating coins means making a fortune, sugar represents sweetness, and cake represents being steadily high. It shows the fisherman's willingness to be auspicious and yearning for wealth. After eating the dumplings, people flocked to the streets, and the street was crowded by the people who watch dragons and fishermen's Yangko.

渔家的大年异常火爆，到处是祥和、热烈的景象。旅客一家老少坐在渔家热炕头上，品尝渔家年饭，体验海岛风土人情，可谓其乐融融。

The fisherman's New Year is extremely hot, and there are peaceful and warm scenes everywhere. Tourists and families of all ages sit on one end of kang, which is near the heating source, taste the fisherman's New Year meal, and experience the customs of the island.

思考与实践

Thinking and practice

参观渔家乐业户,谈谈长岛渔家乐有什么特点?

Visit the fisher's homes and talk about what's the characteristics of Changdao Fisherman home?

你能说说渔家乐还有哪些可以改进的办法吗?

Can you tell us what else methods can be used to improve for Fisherman's Holiday Tour?

第五单元　民间传说

Unit 5　Folklore

长岛历史悠久,有着灿烂的古代文化。"海上仙山""八仙过海""海神娘娘"等传说为缥缈神秘的海岛增色不少,成为游客敬仰和神往的地方。

Changdao has a long history and a splendid ancient culture. Legends such as "Fairy Mountain on the Sea", "Eight Immortals Crossing the Se", and "The Empress of the Sea God" have added a lot to the mysterious island and make it become a place of admiration and fascination for tourists.

图 4-4-1　渔家过大年

第一课　八仙过海
Lesson 1　The Eight Immortals Cross the Sea

　　庙岛群岛,在很早以前叫沙门岛。宋朝初年,这里是朝廷囚禁犯人的地方。《登州府志》有这样的记载:"《宋太宗本纪》建安三年索内外军中不律者发配沙门"。为了看守犯人,宋朝还在岛上修筑了沙门砦,派驻了一部分官兵。这沙门岛是一群孤岛,四面环海,远离大陆。犯人被押进岛来,很难逃离出去。

　　Temple Island Archipelago was called Shamen Island long time ago. In the early years of the Song Dynasty, it was the place where the prisoners were locked up by imperial court. "Records of Dengzhou Fu" has listed: "The Book of Emperor Taizong of the Song Dynasty" in the third year of Jian'an, the irregulars in the military will be distributed to Shamen. In order to guard the prisoners, also Shamen Stockade was built on the island in the Song Dynasty and some officers and soldiers were stationed. The Shamen Island is a group of isolated islands, surrounded by the sea on all sides, far away from the landmass. The prisoners were taken into the island and difficult to escape.

　　朝廷每年只拨给三百人的口粮,犯人日渐增多,口粮便不够吃的。守砦的头目李庆便想出个狠毒的办法,当犯人超过三百人时,便把那些老弱病残者捆住手脚,扔进大海。那些侥幸活下来的,也不比死了舒坦。李庆和看押官兵们稍有不满意,便鞭抽棍打,无情虐待,整个岛上天天闻哭声,日日见死人。两年时间竟死700多人。为了活命,经常有渡海逃生者,均不得成。有个姓吕的壮年汉子,原是领兵打仗的将军,他为人正直,心地善良,足智多谋,敢想敢干。一次朝廷命他带兵去征讨起义造反的义军,仗打胜了,义军的头领也被擒住了,可他念那头目杀赃官,济穷人,光明磊落,行侠仗义,就把他悄悄地放了。皇帝知道后,就将姓吕的革职,发配到沙门岛来。这位将军侠义、英武、血气方刚,早已对朝廷不满,看不惯看守的胡作非为。就私下鼓动众囚犯："咱在这里等死,意思不明逃离？逃出去拣条命,就是逃不出去,咱也是争气鬼,横竖比死在这里当窝囊废强。"他这一席话,立即有六个犯人响应,他们有白发如霜的,有瘸腿拄拐的,有打呱嗒板吹笛弄箫卖唱的,有的还是皇亲国戚。他们齐聚在大黑山岛龙爪山下的海蚀洞里秘密谋划,各人找来葫芦、船板、木棒、驴皮等做抓手和漂浮物,准备选一个月黑风平浪静的晚上,逃往蓬莱大陆。

The imperial court only allocated rations to 300 people each year, and the number of prisoners was increasing, and the rations were not enough. Li Qing, the leader for guard of the stockade, came up with a vicious way. When the number of prisoners exceeded 300, he would tied up the hands and feet of the old, weak, sick and thrown them into the sea. Those who survived by chance were no better than death. Li Qing and its officers and soldiers would beat prisoners with whips and cruelly tortured them as long as feeling dissatisfied. The crying can be heard every day on the island, and dead people could be seen everyday. More than 700 people died in two years. In order to survive, some of them often went cross the sea to escape,but no one succeeded. There was a middle-aged man whose family name was Lv, originally a general, for leading troops in battle. He was upright, kind-hearted, resourceful, and daring to think and do. Once the imperial court ordered him to lead troops to conquer the rebellious rebels, he won the battle. The leader of the rebels was captured, but Lv thought that the leader had killed corrupted officials, helped the poor, was a chivalrous man, so he let him go. After the emperor knew about it, he dismissed Lv and sent him to Shamen Island. This general was chivalrous, heroic and full-blooded. He had long been dissatisfied with the court and detested the guards' abuses. He privately agitated the prisoners: "Comparing with waiting for death here, we had better catch up with the idea to escape? If we escape and choose our lives, we will win credit for oureslves even if we fail. It is better than death here to be useless." he said. Six prisoners responded immediately. Some of them had white hair, some were lame and walked by crutches, some used to playing and singing for living, and some were relatives of the emperor. They gathered in the sea cave under dragon claw Mountain on

Daheishan Island to make secret plans. Everyone brought gourds, boat boards, wooden sticks, donkey skins, etc. as grabs and floats, and prepared to choose a dark and calm night to escape Penglai mainland.

为了不被发现,他们除了在一个大洞里(现叫聚佩洞)议事准备外,暂时分住在另外七个洞里。他们的多次议事和准备,被住在另一个洞里的姓何的姑娘得知,就在他们要起事动手的晚上,她拿着大木盆,跪在众人的面前,苦苦哀求大伙带她逃出火炕。原来她家住青州。这年,当兵的哥哥因思念生病的父母逃回家中,被官兵发现后,发配沙门岛,妹妹紧追不舍,也被官兵押上岛来。进岛不久,哥哥就被看守的官兵活活打死。李庆见姑娘长得俊气,多次强逼她做压砦夫人,定好明日就要拜堂成亲,这姑娘边哭边说,最后道:"你们的动向,俺早就知道,俺死也不做那畜生的老婆,你们就带俺走吧!"见姑娘说得凄惨,大伙听了动心。那姓吕的汉子说:"好姑娘,大伙和你一样命苦,只是蓬莱老远的水路,你咋过得去?"那姑娘指着大木盆说:"这个你们不用愁,俺早就操持好了这玩意,俺就坐在这里漂流过去"!

In order not to be discovered, they lived in other seven caves separately for the time being, apart from being in a big cave (now called Jupei cave) for discussion. Many discussions and preparations were heard by a girl named He, who lived in another cave. On the night, when they were about to start the incident, she took the big tub and knelt in front of everyone, begging everyone to take it for escaping. It turns out that she lives in Qingzhou. This year, her brother (a soldier)fled to home because he missed his sick parents. After being discovered by the officers and soldiers, he was sent to Salmon Island. She was chasing after him and also taken to the island by soldiers. Soon after entering the island, his brother was beaten to death by the guards. Seeing that the girl was beautiful, Li Qing repeatedly forced her to be his wife, and the wedding would be held tomorrow. The girl cried and said at last: "I have known your movements a long time ago, and I will not marry the beast even if died. I beg youto take me away!" The girl said miserably, everyone was touched. The man surnamed Lu said, "Good girl, everyone has the same fate as you. It's just the long waterway in Penglai. How can you get there?" The girl pointed to the big tub and said, "You don't have to worry about this. I have prepared it long ago. I just sit on and drift over by it!"

众人见她说得有理,便一起行动,摸黑杀死了两个看守的官兵,各持物器,跳入海中,朝着南面有灯光的地方游去。一路上,大家你推我拥,我帮他助,终于游到蓬莱丹崖山下,在狮子洞(后称仙人洞)里躲起来。第二天,这八位过海的能人被当地渔民发现,看见他们衣衫褴褛的样子,非常惊奇,于是就问:"你们从什么地方来?"他们顺手一指长岛方向,众渔民惊道:"是从仙岛上来的呀!那又是怎么过渡的呢?"他们又指了指放在洞外的一些器物。那打鱼人更惊奇了:"哎哟哟,你们老的老,瘸的瘸,还有体弱的妇女,就凭这些东西过了大海,不是神就是仙,咱快点报告官府,仙岛上的神仙下凡到咱登州地界啦!"

When everyone saw that she was right, they acted together and killed the two guards in the dark, each holding their objects, jumping into the sea, and swimming towards the lighted area in the south. Along the way, everyone offered support to each other. Finally, they swam to the foot of Penglai Danya Mountain and hid in the Lion Cave (later called Xianren Cave). The next day, the eight men who had crossed the sea were spotted by the local fishermen. They were very surprised when they saw their ragged clothes. They asked, "Where are you from?" They pointed towards Changdao, and the fishermen were surprised. "You came from Fairy Island! How did you come across the sea?" They pointed to some artifacts placed outside the cave. The fisherman was even more surprised: "Oh, look at you, the old, lame, and frail women, rely on these things to cross the sea, You must be either gods or immortals. Let's report to the officials, the gods on the fairy island descended to the realm of Dengzhou!"

众渔民急忙离去,这八个人却害怕起来。有的说:现在官府腐败,咱是流放的逃犯,与其在这个地方等死,不如找些修炼的去处,到民间多做好事,让后人记住咱们,不枉为人来世一场。大家非常赞同他的意见,于是,八个人分赴八个方向,寻迹访师,修炼道行去了。一晃就是百年,他们苦心修炼,成仙得道,为民间百姓做了诸多善事好事。一日,八位仙人在蓬莱的八仙洞里不期而遇,久别重逢,互道思念之情,围着八仙桌开怀畅饮起来,酒助人兴,话语滔滔。回想起当年逃离沙门岛之事,无不感慨万千。如今功成名就,何不旧地重游,以铲除邪恶,救人于水深火海,开创那海上仙山之盛景,造福于岛上黎民百姓。说去便行。有的说："如今咱们过海，各显神通若何？"众仙齐声赞同。于是，浩海云天之中，便呈现出一幅八大仙人借助法宝飘然过海的长卷。

The fishermen hurriedly left, but the eight people became frightened. Some said the feudal officials were corrupt, we were fugitives exiled. Instead of waiting to die in this place, it was better to find some places to practice, to do good things to the people, so that future generations will remember us and we will not be in vain. Everyone agreed with him very much, so the eight people were divided into eight directions, looked for the teacher, and practiced Taoism. A hundred years in a flash. They cultivated painstakingly, became immortals, and did many good deeds for people. One day, the eight immortals met unexpectedly in the Eight Immortals Cave in Penglai. They reunited after a long time and exchanged thoughts. They drank happily around the table of the Eight Immortals, and the words were eloquent. Thinking back to the incident of escaping from Salmon Island, all were filled with emotion. Now we were successful, why not revisited the old days to eradicate evil, save people from misery, create the grand scenery of fairy mountains on the sea, and benefit the people on the island. Just do as you say. Some said: "Now that we cross the sea, how can we show our supernatural powers?" The immortals agreed in unison. As a result, in the vast sea of clouds, there was a long scroll of the Eight Great Immortals flying across the sea with the help of magic weapons.

那汉钟离最是性急，把大芭蕉扇往海里一扔，袒胸露腹，仰躺在蒲席大的扇子上，悠然自得地向庙岛方向漂去。何仙姑眼明手快，将荷花往水中一抛，红光一闪，大如磨盘，仙姑亭亭玉立在花蕊中，随波漂荡。铁拐李的宝葫芦、曹国舅的云板、韩湘子的洞箫、蓝采和的花篮，皆在水中膨大、乘坐的各位仙人也自由自在地驶向前方。张国老的法术让人称奇，箱中取得一撮折叠如厚纸般的驴皮，以水噀之，还成白驴，仙人倒骑着它，踩波踏浪疾行。七仙飞离远去，这吕洞宾一声"去也"！手中宝剑一指，左手拂尘轻甩，霎时海水分开，仙人犹如平地飞行，赶在诸仙之前，转眼之间，已先登达庙岛仙山之上。待众仙上得岛来，大家互相查看，八位身上竟无一点水珠。于是开怀大笑起来。

Han Zhongli was the most impatient. He threw the big banana fan into the sea, exposed his chest, laid his back on the big fan, and drifted towards the temple island in a leisurely manner. He Xiangu was very nimble, and thrown the lotus into the wate; as the red light flashed, the lotus became as big as a grinding plate, Xiangu stood in the stamen, drifted with the waves. Li Tieguai 's treasure gourd, Cao Guojiu's cloud board, Han Xiangzi's vertical bamboo flute, and Luan Caihe's flower basket were all swelling in the water, and the immortals were also free to drive forward. Zhang Guolao's magic arts are amazing. A piece of donkey skin folded like thick paper was obtained from the box, which was choked with water and turned into a white donkey. He rode on it backwards, stepped on the waves and rushed along the waves. The Seven Immortals flew away, and Lu Dongbin said, "Go!" With his treasured sword pointed and his whisk swung by his left hand, the water separated instantly, and he was flying on the ground like a flat ground. Before the immortals, in a flash, he had already landed on the island. Above the fairy mountain, when the immortals came to the island, everyone checked each other, and there was no drop of water on the eight people. So they bursted into laughter.

八仙过海，今非昔比，海上的群岛，也时过境迁。全不见，衣着褴褛的囚犯和面目凶残的守兵；都不闻，打骂驱赶之声和哭喊呻吟之音。再看那诸岛，虽山青水碧，鸟语花香，却是少有人烟，缺少可耕种之田地，也无多能捕捉的鱼虾，仙岛尚需世人辛勤地劳作，更要我等众仙的神助。于是，八仙人略施巧计，驱除那肆意兴风作浪的海妖水怪；广展法力，那些倭寇海贼不敢再来侵岛扰民。为这一方水土的长久生计，八大仙各持宝器，尽显神通，大闹龙宫宝殿，直搅闹得四海龙宫，昼夜毋宁，龙王诸族寝食不安。诸龙王百般无奈，只得下令，四海鱼群虾族春来冬去，须经仙岛水道，迴游整个渤海，使渤海成为四季鱼腾虾跃的大渔场。数十年间，帆来船往，海市兴隆。许多大陆人们从四面八方迁来这海上群岛，在辽阔的渤黄海捞金挖银，在漫长的海边滩涂采玉拾宝，仙岛便日益昌盛繁荣起来。

The Eight Immortals had crossed the sea, and the islands on the sea had also changed over time. None of the prisoners in ragged clothes and the brutal guards could be seen and none of the sounds of beatings, scolding, and moans be heard. Looking at the islands, although the mountains and the waters were green, the birds sang and the flowers were fragrant, but there were few people, there was no arable land, and there were not many fish and shrimps that can be caught. The fairy island still needed the hard work of the people of the world. Therefore, the Eight Immortals used tricks to get rid of the sea monsters that wantonly stirred up troubles, and spread their magic power, in this way, the Japanese pirates dared not to invade the island again to disturb the people. For the long-term livelihood of this land and water, the eight great immortals held their treasures and showed their magical powers, created tremendous in the Dragon Palace Palace, stirred up the Dragon Palace in the four seas, making them restless day and night. The dragon kings were helpless in every way, so they had to order that the four seas of fish and shrimp clan will go through the fairy island waterway in spring and winter, and travel back to the entire Bohai Sea, making the Bohai sea a large fishing ground. For decades, the sea had been prospering with sails coming and going. Many people from the mainland had moved to this maritime archipelago from all directions, dug for gold and silver in the vast Bohai Sea, and dug for jade and treasures in the long beaches of the sea, and the fairy island had become increasingly prosperous.

　　仙人闲暇无事，也遍游大小三十余岛、礁。尽览海上仙山之风光。转眼又是百年，长山列岛处处留下了他们的神祇仙迹，也流传着八大仙人的趣闻佳话。大黑山岛的龙爪山下的九仙神洞，他们当年寝居和议事之地仍然安在。走进"议事厅"的大洞里，仿佛还能听到他们商计对策的说话声。仙姑洞里，何仙姑就寝床边的一块鞋状大石头，据说是仙姑当年落下的绣鞋，日久膨大而成。在张果老住室的海边，有一槽形的巨石，传说是他喂驴的石槽，里面的水藻海菜，那是神驴的草料。在北长山岛西端，珍珠门内的九丈崖下的醉仙石，是汉钟离酒醉纳凉酣睡的佳处；那块龙舌礁更有来历，据说是龙王镇海之宝，是吕洞宾得胜归来，顺手扔于此地；龙舌礁上，韩湘子"横箫洞吹，吟风弄浪"，充满了浪漫情调，棋盘礁上，曹国舅和铁拐李，择此佳处，对弈比武，又是何等雅致。传说有一次，汉钟离硬要参战，可他下得急，输得快，连输五盘，他一气之下，抓起一把棋子向大海扬去。这一举止虽不文雅，但从此以后，在这片海域里长出的"将军礁""马抢石""车由岛"和"双卒山"，至今仍在，为"海上仙山"又添景趣。

The immortals had nothing to do, and they traveled around more than 30 islands and reefs, taking a panoramic view of the scenery of the fairy mountains on the sea. In a blink of an eye, it was another hundred years, and their traces were left on the island everywhere, and there were also anecdotal stories about the Eight Immortals. The Nine Immortal Caves under Longzhua Mountain on Daheishan Island, where they lived and discussed matters at that time was still there. Walking into the big cave where they discussed before, it seemed that their voices for discussing countermeasures cound still be heard. In Xiangu Cave, there was a large shoe-like rock beside the bed where He Xiangu was sleeping was said to be the embroidered shoes that Xiangu left here in the past, which had grown over time. There was a trough-shaped boulder at the seaside of Zhang Guolao's residence. According to legend, it was the stone trough where he feeds the donkey. The algae and sea vegetables in it were fodder for the god donkey. At the western end of North Changshan Island, the Drunken Immortal Stone under the Jiuzhang Cliff in the Pearl Gate was a good place for Hanzhongli to drink and enjoy the cool sleep. The dragon tongue reef had more origins, and it was said to be the treasure used by the Dragon King for protection of the sea, and it was left by Lv Dongbin after victory. On the Dragon Tongue Reef, Han Xiangzi "blowed in the Hengxiao care, chanted the wind and waves", full of romance. On the chessboard reef, Cao Guojiu and Tieguai Li chose this best place to play. How elegant was the competition. Legend had it that once, Han Zhongli insisted on participating in a competition, but he played anxiously, lost quickly, and lost five games in a row. In a fit of anger, he grabbed a handful of chess piece and threw them towards the sea. Although this behavior was not elegant, since then, the "General Reef", "Maqiang Shuangzu Stone", "Cheyou Island" and "Shuangshou Mountain" that had grown in this sea area were still there today, adding new sceneries for the "Fair Mountain on the Sea.

思考与实践

Thinking and practice
复述课文主要内容。
Retell the main content of the text.

第二课　海神娘娘的传说

Lesson 2　The Legend of the Sea God Empress

　　相传在宋朝初年,福建省蒲田县海边的一个小渔村,住着一户姓林的渔民。生得一男一女。女儿在农历三月二十三日出生后,月余不会啼哭,父母便起名"默娘"。她自幼好学,聪明过人,8 岁从师读经,过目成诵,闻一知十。虽生长在渔村,却偏吃素食,从不杀生吃荤,猪羊鸡鸭,渔虾蟹贝,一概不食,只吃五谷杂粮,鲜果蔬菜,特别喜食海藻菜类,饮雨雪露水,虽体态纤弱,却水性极好,潮汐气象不学自通。为人心地善良,乐于助人。风浪天,独驾小舟,为渔家抢险排难,救死扶伤。深受渔家村人的爱戴。

According to legend, in the early years of the Song Dynasty, there lived a family of fishermen named Lin in a small fishing village by the sea in Putian County, Fujian Province. a boy and a girl were given birth to. The daughter was born on the twenty-third of the third month of the lunar calendar, but she could not cry since birthed for more than a month, so her parents named her "Mo Niang". She was studious since she was a child, and very smart. She read the scriptures according to the instruction of a teacher when she was 8 years old. Although he grew in a fishing village, he preferred to eat vegetarian food. He never killed meat, pigs, lambs, chickens, ducks, fish, shrimps, crabs and shellfish. He only ate whole grains, fresh fruits and vegetables. He especially liked seaweed and vegetables. Drinking rain, snow and dew. Although she was weak, but at swimming; very good, she self learnt the knowledge such as tide and meterology. He was kind-hearted and helpful. In stormy weather, alone in a small boat, he rescued fishermen and the wounded and was loved by the people of Yujia Village.

　　一天,默娘的父兄出海打鱼,她和母亲正在家做饭,天气突然变了,天空黑云翻滚,大风骤起,巨浪翻涌,雷雨交加,正在烧火的默娘却恍似沉沉睡去。母亲见她睡中咬紧牙关,蹙着双目,手扒脚蹬,一副拼命挣扎的状态,非常吃惊,"默娘、默娘……"连喊数声,她也不醒,便使劲推她几下,她才猛然醒来。连叫"不好、不好!"母亲惊问:"我儿,出了何事?"女儿戚然应道:"刚才女儿梦见父、兄在海里翻船落水,女儿手拉着哥哥,口咬着爹爹,正向岸边拼命游来,母亲突然推我,不由得张口'啊'了一声,似把爹爹丢了,只救得哥哥。爹爹怕是凶多吉少了。"说完,泪珠涟涟。母亲急道:"我儿不要胡思乱说,时候不早,快去海边看他们回来没有?"默娘刚要出门,只见哥哥浑身是水,万分悲痛地进门,扑倒在母亲面前,哭诉道:"我和爹爹正在拖网扑鱼,天气突变,海面风大浪高,爹爹砍断网缆,我们摇橹加棹,紧急收港,可风越刮越大,两三个巨浪,就把船掀翻了,我们一摔进风浪窝里,不大一会就浑身无力,游不动了。这时就觉得有人拽着我的衣服往岸上拖。开始爹爹和我还在一起,不知什么时候,爹爹不见了。天黑了,我上了岸,到处找爹爹也没找到,只得回来。"默娘妈哭得死去活来,全家家披麻戴孝,发送了爹爹。

One day, Mo Niang's father and brother went fishing at sea. She and her mother were cooking at home. The weather suddenly changed. The sky was dark and clouds rolled, strong winds rose, huge waves and thunderstorms surged, but Mo Niang who was making a fire seemed to fall asleep. Her mother saw her clenching her teeth while sleeping, her eyes frowned, her hands stomped on her feet, and her struggled desperately, her mother was very surprised, "Mo Niang, Mo Niang..." She didn't show any respense after being shouted for several times. After being pushed hard a few times, she woke up suddenly. "Not good, not good!" The mother asked in surprise, "My child, what's wrong?" The daughter replied, "Just now I dreamed that his father and brother were overturned in the sea, and I was holding my brother and biting my father. I was swimming desperately towards the shore, when you suddenly pushed me, and she couldn't help but open my mouth, as if lost Daddy, and only saved my brother. I was afraid that my father would be dead." After finishing, tears were dripping. Mother said anxiously: "My child, don't talk nonsense. It was not early. Go to the beach and see if they are back." Mo Niang was about to go out, but her brother entered the door with great grief and fell in front of her mother. Cried, "when my dad and I are trawling the fish, the weather has changed suddenly, the sea is windy and the waves are high, and daddy cut the nets, we shook the sculls and rushed to the port, but the wind was getting bigger and bigger, and two or three huge waves made the boat overturned, and as soon as we fell into the center of stormy wave, we were weak and unable to swim for a while. At this time, we felt that someone was dragging my clothes onto the shore. At first, daddy was still together with me, I don't know when daddy disappeared. When it got dark, I went ashore and looked for Daddy everywhere, but failed and I had to come back." Mo Niang's mother was crying so hard, and the whole family was putting on mourning apparel for their relative.

　　母亲知道女儿不是"凡人"。"默娘救亲"的故事也慢慢地在渔村传播开来。许多船家渔民想起往日遭风遇难，总好像有灯引路，有人推送，遂得脱险平安。便议论猜测，那必是默娘所为，纷纷前往拜谢，祈求保佑。一时门庭若市，消息传遍沿海及诸岛，惊动地方官府。天机一经泄露，默娘自知将不久于人世。便对哥哥道出实情："我本是东海龙王之女，脱离龙宫，下凡人世，为的是济危救难。现在人皆知我，凡身便再难生活于世上。近日，我多次梦游神往北方一处宝地，意在那里留居升天，便我济难助人，普救众生，望兄助我！"

　　The mother knew that her daughter was not "common people." The story of "Mo Niang Rescue" also spread gradually in the fishing village. Many boatmen and fishermen remembered that they were in danger they were in the past, It always seemed that there was a light to guide their way; and they were pushed, and escaped from danger. Then they discussed and guessed that it must have been the work of Mo Niang, and they went to worship and pray for blessing. For a while, the news spread all over the coast and the islands, alarming the local government. Once the secret was leaked, Mo Niang knew that she would die soon. He told his brother the truth: "I was originally the daughter of the Dragon King of the East China Sea. I left the Dragon Palace and went to the mortal world for relief. Now everyone knows me, it will be difficult for me to live in the world. Recently, I have repeatedly dreamed about a fascinated treasure land in the north, intending to stay there and ascend to heaven, so that I can help others, and save all living beings, but hope that you will help me!"

　　于是，兄妹驾一小舟，沿漫长海岸线，晓行夜宿，朔北而上。渡过长江口，穿越连云港，开进胶州湾，却不见宝地踪影，驶过"天尽头"，进了龙须湾，不是意中的佳处；看过养马岛，驻足芝罘山，观望烟台山，亦非仙山良居。船过老爷山，远望黄渤海交汇处的一列群岛上空，紫光笼罩，瑞气缭绕，峰峦清幽，岩涧陡峻，松柏参天，修竹茂密。默娘虽未到过此地，却好像似梦中所见，旧日所想的仙山佳处。兄妹急忙赶进群岛，环游数岛，但见居中一小岛，仿佛是一只巨大的五彩的凤凰，静卧水中。默娘轻移蓬步，登上仙境，但见岛上云遮翠岭，雾障清峦，曲水流响如韵，松竹碧绿欲滴，特别是站在那"凤凰"的脖子上，前后两山夹一川，左右海水分两色，格外清丽敞亮。抬头望，天空透清碧兰；看脚下，海水平静墨绿。放眼四周，东有南、北长山岛，西邻大、小黑山岛，北对一线排列着的猴矶、瑭琅诸岛礁，南望远山的蓬莱大陆，群岛环抱这一辽阔的海湾碧塘，可锚泊成千上万船只，而不受风掀浪涌之扰，岛礁之间尚有五六个海域通道，伸向四面八方，广连五湖四海。这一天然良港福湾，更是普度众生，保佑南来北往船只免遭劫难的好地方。

　　So they drove a small boat along the long coastline, stayed overnight at dawn, and headed northward. Crossing the Yangtze River estuary, crossing Lianyungang, and driving into Jiaozhou Bay, but there was no trace of the treasure land, driving past the "end of the sky" and entering Longxu Bay, which was not the ideal place. they had seen Yangma Island, stopped at Zhifu Mountain and watched Yantai Mountain, all of which were not good places for stay. The ship passed the Laoye Mountain, looked far over a series of islands at the confluence of the Yellow River and Bohai sea, where shrouded in purple light, surrounded by propitious vapors, quiet peaks, steep rock and rovine, towered pines and cypresses, and densely cultivated bamboos. Although Mo Niang had never been here, it seemed to be the best place seen in the dream and thought of in the past. They hurried into the archipelago and traveled around several islands, but saw a small island in the middle which was like a huge colorful phoenix lying still in the water. Mo Niang moved lightly and stepped onto the fairyland, but she saw the clouds covering the green ridges on the island, the fog barriers and clear ridges, the curving waters resounded like rhyme, and green pine and bamboo, especially standing on the neck of the "phoenix"; you would see that the mountains were surrounded by a river, and the left and right seas had two colors, which were particularly clear and bright. When looked up, the sky was clear and blue. When looked at my feet, the sea was calm and dark green. Looking around, there were northern and southern Changshan Island in the east. Daheishan Island and Xiaoheishan Island were in the west. In the bay and green ponds Bitang, thousands of ships can be anchored without being disturbed by winds and surges. There were five or six sea passages between the islands and reefs, which extended in all directions and went to all corners of the world. This natural and good harbor, was a good place for all living beings to be protected from disasters.

福祉选定，默娘向兄长道别："哥哥快回老家，代我在母亲面前多尽孝道。我虽不在你们身边，但魂灵永随左右。今后，你们有啥急难之事，只要喊我三声，我会即到相助。我在此宝岛良湾，坐守黄渤海要道，外通五湖四海，静心致志为船家渔民排险解难，随我终生夙愿。"说完便闭目静坐，不吃不喝，无声无息，打坐三日，化为一尊石像。远近船家渔民闻讯，齐聚小岛，焚香烧纸，顶礼膜拜。积极响应倡导者，纷纷捐金集资，建造一座庙宇，供奉着默娘的石像，尊为海神娘娘。从此，神庙名扬四海，传遍神州。小岛也因此叫作"庙岛"。

Mo Niang said goodbye to her brother after choosing the place of happiness: "Brother, go back to my hometown and do more of my filial piety in front of my mother. Although I am not by your side, my soul will always be there. From now on, if you have any urgent matters, just call me three times. I will come to help you right away. The place I chose here was the main road of the Yellow Sea and Bohai, connecting all over the world, and I am dedicated to helping the boatmen and fishermen to remove dangers and solve problems. I will follow my lifelong wishes." After saying that, she closed eyes and sat down; she did not eat or drink, and she meditated for three days and turned into a stone statue. Upon hearing the news, boatmen and fishermen from far and near gathered on the island, burned incense and paper, and worshiped. Actively responding to the calls, they donated money to raise funds to build a temple with a stone statue of Mo Niang, revered as the Sea God Empress. Since then, the temple had become famous all over China. The small island was also called "Temple Island".

宋徽宗宣和四年 (1122 年)，福建的商会名士不远万里，追寻而来，在庙岛重修了娘娘神庙——天后宫，精塑娘娘金身。

In the forth year of Emperor Huizong Xuanhe of the Song Dynasty (1122), the celebrities of the Fujian Chamber of Commerce came here from far and wide. They rebuilt the Empress Temple, Tianhou Palace, on Miaodao, and refined the golden body of the Empress.

海神娘娘升天以后，乘风踏浪，灵游四海，普救众生。哪里有难，她便哪里显灵，哪里遭灾，她便哪里出现。娘娘显灵救难，祖祖辈辈，家喻户晓。海难中求助于娘娘，更是人们战胜劫难的一种精神力量，四海船家无不对海神娘娘虔诚恭敬。传说最多最广的当数海难中"娘娘赐灯"保佑的故事。每当狂风肆虐，恶浪排空，天海难分，黑暗无边的危难时刻。船只遇难，只要连喊三声："娘娘保佑"！那船头的不远处，准有一盏红灯，仿佛是娘娘擎灯引路，船头前面，即刻闪开一条金光平静的海水通道，跟着红灯走，沿着金光行，总能化险为夷，安全抵达海岸，就是再大的风浪，也保准平安无事。在无数海岛渔村里，更有"娘娘歌舞镇风浪"的传说。每当海上风起浪涌，海难天灾临头，船只遇险未归之际，渔村老少便拥向海边，跪拜滩头，焚香烧纸，为出海亲人祈保平安。高声喊着："娘娘保佑！"海神便乘风驾云，赶到海边，轻声吟唱，翩翩起舞，说来也怪，海神的歌声传开，风便悄悄地息了；海神的裙裾飘过，浪便慢慢地平了，海上的亲人便好生生地回岸归港了。类似的传说故事，数不胜数，与日俱增，在船家渔民中，祖祖辈辈，延绵不断，越说越多，越传越广，越讲越神。在长岛县的北五乡镇，至今仍有健在的老人，能活灵活现地讲述当年亲身经历过的海难中得到娘娘的救助和为亲人祈祷而受到娘娘的荫护，平安脱险的真实故事。这也正是天后宫建庙以来，历朝各代，一修再修，四海船家，八方渔民，对海神娘娘顶礼膜拜，近千年香火不断的缘故。

After ascending to heaven, the Seagod Empress rode the wind and waves, traveled all over the world, and saved all living beings. Wherever there was trouble, she would show up there, and wherever suffered by disasters, she would also be there. The empress had appeared for rescue, and been well-known for generations. Asking for help from Niang Niang in a shipwreck was rather a spiritual force for people to overcome the catastrophe. The boatmen from all over the world were all respectful to Niang Niang, the sea god. The most legendary story was "The Empress Giving Light" in a shipwreck. Whenever the wind was raging, the waves were surging, the sky and the sea were inseparable, and the darkness was boundless. If the ship was in danger, you only needed to shout three times in a row: "Miangniang Bless!" Not far from the bow, there must be a red light, as if a lady was holding a light to lead the way. In front of the bow, a golden light and calm sea channel flashed out immediately. Following the red light and walking along the golden light will make you reach safe place. Arriving at the coast, no matter how big the wind and waves were, it will be safe and sound. In countless fishing villages on the islands, there was even a legend of "The Singing and Dancing suppress Wind and Waves". Whenever the sea winded and surged, the shipwreck was imminent, and the ship was in danger but had not returned, the young and old in the fishing village will rush to the beach, bowed down on the beach, burnt incense and paper, and prayed for the safety of their relatives on the sea. Yelling loudly: "May bless me!" The sea god rode on the wind and drove to the beach, sang softly, and danced lightly, which was strange to say, when the seagod's song spread, the wind quietly became calm. The seagod's skirt fluttered. After that, the waves calmed down slowly, and their relatives on the sea returned to port alive and well. There were countless similar legends and stories, and they were increasing day by day and continued for generationsof fishrmen. The more they talked, the more they spread, and the more miraculous they talked about them. In the North Five Townships of Changdao County, there were still alive old people who can vividly tell the true story of being rescued by the empress during the shipwreck and praying for the relatives and being protected by the God. This was also the reason why since the God was built in Tianhou Palace, it had been repaired by all dynasties; and the fishermen from all over the world, endlessly worshipped the god of the sea, and the incense had continued for nearly a thousand years.

思考与实践

Thinking and practice

讲述几件海神娘娘的传奇故事。

Telling a few legendary stories of the Seagod Empress.

第三课 唐王东征的故事

Lesson 3 The story of Eastward Expedition by the Emperor of Tang Dynasty

庙岛群岛（长山列岛）横亘于我国内海一渤海的出口处,地理位置十分险要,是海上的军事重地。早在大唐贞观年间就成为唐朝跨海东征,拓边安邦的一条重要海上通道,时至一千多年后的今天,这里不仅留有唐军东渡征战时的遗址遗迹,还广泛地流传着一些关于唐太宗东征的故事传说。

The Miaodao Archipelago (Changshan Archipelago) lies at the exit of the Bohai, the inland sea of our country. The geographical position is very dangerous, and it is a military center on the sea. As early as in the Zhenguan period of the Tang Dynasty, it became an important sea channel for the Tang Dynasty's cross-sea eastward expedition, and expansion and maintenance of stabilily. Today, more than a thousand years later, there are not only the relics of the Tang army's eastward expedition, but also extensive relics. There are some stories and legends about Tang Taizong's Eastern Expedition.

一宿街

Yi Su Street

大唐初年,唐王李世民率兵跨海东征到达的第一站便是大榭岛（今南长山岛）。上岛后,唐太宗在岛的北部一处山坡前安营扎寨,名曰:南城（今南城村）,派大将尉迟敬德在北长山岛的一处平缓之地安营扎寨,名曰：北城（今北城村）。两城依山面水而筑,遥相呼应对峙,十分雄伟气派。尉迟将军跟随唐王多年征战,功绩显赫,深得唐王的爱戴和信赖。往常在一起时,唐王对尉迟敬德是日必召见，夜必察谈。现时这样一水相隔，无路可通，来回全凭船渡，太宗甚觉不便。

In the early years of the Tang Dynasty, the first stop reached by Emperor Li Shimin, who led his troops across the sea, was Daxie Island (now South Changshan Island). After arriving on the island, Emperor Taizong of Tang set up camp in front of a hillside in the northern part of the island. The name was: Nancheng (now Nancheng Village). General Yuchi Jingde was sent to camp in a gentle place on North Chengshen Island. The name was Beicheng (now Beicheng Village). The two cities were built on mountains and rivers, and they were very majestic. General Yuchi followed the king of Tang for many years in battle, and his achievements were outstanding, and he was deeply loved and trusted by the king of Tang. Before, the king of Tang would summon Yuchi Jingde every day and talked at night. Taizong found it inconvenient to be so separated by the water, and there was no way to go.

一天，太宗闻爱将尉迟敬德得了重病，便好生着急，立即登船前去探望，恰巧这时海上波涛汹涌、水急浪高，只晕得唐太宗翻肠倒胃，呕吐不止。见到尉迟敬德后，太宗道："这回来看你，晕得孤家苦不堪言。若是两岛之间有路可通，何以至此。"

One day, when Taizong heard that the general Yuchi Jingde was seriously ill, he became anxious and immediately boarded the ship to visit. It happened that the sea was rough and the water was high at this time, and Tang Taizong became vomited due to seasickness. After seeing Yuchi Jingde, Taizong said, "I'm so dizzy to see you this time. If there is a road between the two islands, how it is so."

人们常说皇帝金口玉言，他的话被土地爷听到，立即升天，禀报于玉皇大帝，玉帝即命海龙王为太宗拦海造路。

People often said that the emperor had precious words; when his words were heard by the landlord, he immediately ascended to heaven, reported to the Jade Emperor, the Yu Emperor ordered the Sea Dragon King to block the sea for building of road.

龙王的几位太子接受父命，立即召集虾兵蟹将、鱼卒龟勇，做了部署。当天半夜里,本来风平浪静的南北长山岛之间的海域,突然风声大作,浪涛涌动。那成千上万的水族精灵扯风裹浪、各显神通、海底掀沙搬石,搅得山摇地动。第二天一早,那些好奇的兵士到海边一看,只见一条宽阔的卵石大道横跨在碧波之中,将南、北长山连在了一起。兵将把这事奏报唐太宗,太宗高兴地说道:"天知朕意,海随吾愿,好一个'一宿街'也。"打那以后,人们就叫这条海上卵石道为"一宿街"了。后人看那筑路卵石,晶莹如琥珀美玉,也称她"玉石街"。

Several princes of the Dragon King accepted his father's order and immediately summoned shrimp soldiers, crab soldiers, fish soldiers and turtles to make arrangements. In the middle of the night, the sea area between the north and south Changshan Island, which was originally calm, suddenly blew and the waves surged. Thousands of aquarium elves, displayed their magical powers, lifted sand and moved rocks on the bottom of the sea, and stirred the mountains and the ground. Early next morning, those curious soldiers went to the beach and saw a wide pebble avenue spanning the green waves, connecting the north and south Changshan mountains together. The soldiers reported the incident to Emperor Taizong of Tang Dynasty. Taizong happily said, "Heaven knows my wishes, and the sea follows my wishes. What a good 'Yisu street'." After that, people called this sea pebble road 'Yisu Streat'. Later generations looked at the road pebble, crystal clear like amber jade, also called her "Jade Street."

望驾沟
Wangjiagou

唐太宗久驻南城,感到有些枯燥。一日,对身边的文臣武将们说:"众爱卿,孤家近日心中好生烦闷,相伴出游一番如何?"众人齐声赞同,备齐车马,自连城向东沿海边而行。一路上太宗观赏了"望夫礁""老翁钓鱼石"等海上佳景。中午时分,来到了现在的王沟地界。王沟南、北、西三面环山,东临大海。太宗见此地山环水绕,景色秀美,他又仔细观瞻了神宫仙殿般的诸多景观,村里又多有先人(仙人)居住,感叹道:"世人皆知这海上仙山,却不晓得仙境的源头原来在此",便让侍从在"仙境源"上摆好宴席,君臣边饮酒边观看景致。这时天色格外晴朗,向东望去,只见大海中有一小岛,绿树芳草、竹林叠翠,亭阁隐现,海鸟飞鸣,好一幅美丽海上画图!太宗赞叹不已。急问大臣:"前方何处?"大臣道:"乃大竹山岛"。"好个大竹山岛风光,今日乘兴前往畅游一番,岂不更妙!"太宗令下,众随从将士忙准备好龙舟前往。来到大竹山岛一看,果然是个山奇水秀、林木葱茏的好地方。太宗高高兴兴地观赏山水花鸟、竹林和奇礁异石。不觉夜色渐浓,只好同文武大臣宿在了竹林亭阁内,准备在天亮后再返回大榭岛。谁知天有不测风云,接连数日狂风大作、浪高涛猛,船不能行。太宗着急,守在大榭岛的东海边上的文武百官,更是为圣驾担忧,日夜在海边焚香祈祷,盼望圣驾归来。恰巧这日有夜叉巡海,查看到大榭岛东海口,突然看见万人跪拜,祈祷声阵阵,仔细一听原来是祈祷太宗出游平安归来,便急将这事奏知海龙王。海龙王闻后急道:"那太宗乃是一代开国明君,统一华夏,功昭日月。今日又亲率兵将拓边安疆,定要使其平安。"众虾兵蟹将闻命,立即平波息浪,太宗也随之乘船顺利归来。

Tang Taizong was stationed in Nancheng for a long time, feeling a little boring. One day, He said to the civil servants and military commanders around me: "I have been very bored recently, how about traveling together?" Everyone agreed in unison, prepared their carts and horses, and walked from Liancheng to the east coast. Along the way, Taizong watched "Wangfu Reef" and "Old Man Fishing Stone" and other beautiful sea scenes. At noon, they arrived at the places called Wanggou currently. Wanggou was surrounded by mountains in the south, north and west, and faced the sea in the east. Taizong saw that this place was surrounded by mountains and water, and the scenery was beautiful. He took a close look at the many landscapes like shrines and immortals. There were many ancestors (fairies) living in the village. The source of the fairyland was here, so the attendants set up a banquet on the "source of the fairyland", and the monarchs and ministers watched the scenery while drinking. At this time, the sky was particularly clear. Looking east, I saw a small island in the sea, green trees and grasses, bamboo groves, pavilions looming, seabirds flying, and a beautiful picture on the sea. Taizong was amazed. Urgently asked the minister: "Where is the front?" The minister said, "It's Dazhushan Island." "It was a great view of Dazhushan Island. Wouldn't it be better to go for a swim today!" Under Taizong's order, all the entourages and soldiers hurriedly prepared the dragon boat to go. When I came to Dazhushan Island, it turned out to be a good place with beautiful mountains and lush forests. Taizong happily watched landscapes, flowers and birds, bamboo forests and strange reefs. Unconsciously the night was getting darker, he had to stay with the minister of civil and military affairs in the bamboo pavilion, preparing to return to Daxie Island after dawn. Unexpectedly, the sky was unpredictable, and there were violent winds and violent waves for several days, and the boat can't move. Taizong was anxious. The civil and military officials guarding the east coast of Daxie Island were even more worried for the emperor. They burned incense and prayed at the beach day and night, looking forward to the return of the emperor. It just so happened that there was a Yaksha patrolling the sea that day. When it checked the east sea mouth located in Daxie Island, I suddenly saw thousands of people kneeling and praying. When listened carefully, It knew that they were praying for Taizong's safe return from a trip, so it hurried to tell the story of the Sea Dragon King. After hearing this, the Sea Dragon King said anxiously: "Taizong was the founding emperor of a generation, uniting China and making great achievements. Today, he personally led his troops to expand the borders and borders and maintain stability, and it is a make them safe." The shrimp soldiers and crabs heard their orders and immediately made the waves calmed down. After the waves were over, Taizong also returned smoothly by boat.

由于王沟沟口曾经发生成千上万将士跪望圣驾出游归来的事儿,以后人们就称这条沟为"望驾沟"。再后来,又由于语言关系,便把"望驾沟"演变成"王家沟"。直到新中国成立前,才渐渐简称为"王沟"。

Because thousands of soldiers kneeled down and expected emperor's return from a trip in Wanggoukoukou, people will call this ditch "Wangjiagou" in the future. Later, due to language relations, "Wangjiagou" evolved into "Wangjiagou". It was only gradually referred to as "Wanggou" before liberation.

钦岛唐王山唐王井

Qindao Island, Tangwang Mountain, Tangwang Well

一日，风向正好，唐王登龙舟，率三军从大榭岛起营东进，船行半日，前军来报："海天相接之处，云雾缥缈之中，有数岛若隐若现"。唐王传令："三军开赴列岛，扎营休整。"

One day, when the wind was in the right direction, King Tang boarded the dragon boat and led the three armies to march eastward from Daxie Island. The boat went for half a day. The front army reported: "Where the sea and the sky meet, in the misty clouds, several islands are looming." ordered King Tang: "The three armies went to the archipelago, camped and rested."

不多时，上得岛来，只见群山环抱一开阔平地，四周古木参天，百花斗妍，月牙似的几处海湾滩涂，皆玑珠卵石，晶莹剔透，在海浪的冲刷下，沙沙作响，又一番神仙境地。风光虽好，怎奈此时唐王军务紧急，无暇尽意浏览，只得敛气定神，策划安营之事。

Not long after came to the island, they saw an open flat land surrounded by an mountains; the towering ancient trees grown all around, hundreds of flowers blooming, and crescent-like beaches of several bays, all with pearls and pebbles, crystal clear, rustling under the washing of the waves, being regards as another fairyland. Although the scenery was good, the emperor was busy with military affairs, and had no time to browse, and had to gather his breath and plan the camping related affairs.

岛上有一大山十分高陡，唐王要登上山顶观察地势，以便划定三军的布局。遂命军士凿石开山，伐木填涧，修筑御道。大约半个时辰，两条环山道路开成，直达山顶。唐王甚是满意，称下道为大马道，上道为二马道，遂弃船乘马上得山来。站在山巅，极目远望，只见海天一色，微波不兴，令人心旷神怡，望南有一大岛如巨石立水，其状若鼍，当即赐名为"鼍矶岛"（今砣矶岛），令一军前往扎营，作为后应。望北与高句丽相峙处也有两岛，一水相隔，即命前去岛上修筑皇城（后称北隍城岛，南隍城岛），待出击之日唐王好亲临皇城布阵督战。由远及近，环视山下，只见岛中有一宽敞海湾，唐王又命将士加以开拓修筑，成为一处避风良港。由于湾深向好，就是大风浪天港内也平静如镜，称之为"天口"。

There was a large mountain on the island that was very high and steep. King Tang intended to climb to the top to observe the terrain in order to delineate the layout of the three armies. Then the sergeant was ordered to dig into the mountains, cut wood and fill the gully, and build the imperial road. In about half an hour, two roads around the mountain opened up to the top of the mountain. King Tang was very satisfied, calling the lower road the Da Ma Road and the upper road the Er Ma Road, then he rode a horse to get to the top of mountain. Standing on the top of the mountain, looking far away, You'll see the sea melt into sky, and the microwave was kept calm, it was refreshing, and there was a big island like a boulder standing in the water, and its shape was like a bird. It was immediately named "Tuoji Island" (now Tuoji Island) by emperor and an army was to ordered encamp as a follow-up. There were also two islands where Wangbei and Goguryeo faced each other. They were separated by the water. They were ordered to build the imperial city on the island (later called Beihuangcheng Island and Nanhuangcheng Island). On the day of the attack, King Tang will visit the imperial city and supervise the battle. Looking around the mountain from far to near, I saw a spacious bay in the island. King Tang ordered his soldiers to open up and build it to become a shelter from the wind. As the bay was deep and good, even the strong wind and waves in the sky were as calm as a mirror, which was called "Tiankou".

唐王玉居山顶，诸事安排皆妥，唯独用水十分不便，每天需大量人力从山底运送。一日，唐王走出军营，见众多军士挑水攀山，甚是费力。随问从臣，方知原委。立即召见御史，问道："何不掘地取水？"御史答："先时已掘地数处，皆不得水。"唐王听后，哈哈笑道："朕代天立命，凡天下万物，莫不听朕调遣。待朕亲点一处，降旨一道，命其献水是了！"说完便朝脚下指了指："此处掘井，必得水也！"众将士见唐王所指之处，恰处高山之顶，知难有水，无不摇头叹矣。可御旨不可违，只得挖掘起来。挖地数尺后，露出一顽石，御史回奏，唐王到："凿开顽石，便是龙泉。"众将士闻命，奋力凿石，凿着凿着，那顽石轰然一声破裂开来，泉水即刻便"骨碌骨碌"地喷涌而出，那水质清澈甘甜，随驾的官员与众将士无不欢腾雀跃,齐呼万岁。从此以后,由于唐王太宗在岛上下了道道钦命,所以,此岛被人们称为"钦岛";那山因唐王在此居住过,所以称为"唐王山";那井因唐王亲点的地位,所以也就称为"唐王井"了。

King Tang lived on the top of the mountain, and everything was arranged properly, except that the water was very inconvenient to be obtained, and a lot of manpower was needed to transport it from the bottom of the mountain every day. One day, King Tang walked out of the barracks and saw many sergeants carrying water and climbing mountains, which was very laborious. Asking the ministers to know the whole story. He immediately summoned senior officers and asked: "Why don't you dig the ground for water?" and replied: "We have dug a few places in the first place, and there is no water." After king Tang heard this, he laughed and said: "All things, must listen to my dispatch. and the doors I pointed out will have water!" After saying that, he pointed to his feet: "If you dig a well here, you will get water!" All the soldiers saw Tang. The place where the king pointed was right on the top of the mountain, knowing that there was no water, all shook head and sighed. But the imperial decree cannot be violated, so they had to dig it up. After digging the ground a few feet, a hard stone was exposed. Yushi replied, and the king of Tang said: "Chisel the hard stone, and the spring water was just under it." The soldiers heard the orders, chiseled the stone, and it is broken loudly. When it bursted, the spring water spewed out immediately. The quality of the water was clear and sweet. The officials and soldiers who drove along were all cheering and shouting for joy. From then on, due to Emperor Taizong of the Tang Dynasty on the island, the island was called "Qin Island", the mountain was called "Tangwang Mountain" because of the 'King kang's' residence. As the position of well is selected by King Tang so it was also called "Tangwangjing".

沧海桑田,千年巨变。现在,天口已被沙石淤平,埋于地下,然"唐王山"的"大马道""二马道"犹在,"唐王井"残迹仍存,只是井水已经干涸,井壁已坍塌罢了。

Time brings a great change to the world. At present, the Tiankou had been silted with sands and stones and buried underground, but the "Da Ma Road" and "Er

Ma Road" of "Tangwang Mountain" were still there, and the remaining trace of "Tangwang Well" were still there, but the well had dried up and the well walls had been collapsed.

巡海将军——印鱼
General Patrol-Seal Fish

唐太宗率军继续渡海东征。一日，船队行至南、北隍城岛附近，举目望去，见两岛笼罩在一片淡淡的薄雾之中，山峰迭出，秀丽如画。山坳里露出几处茅舍，升起缕缕炊烟。偶有渔家姑娘在山涧小径上出现，飘然欲飞，真如仙境一般。

Emperor Taizong led his army to continue to cross the sea and march eastward. One day, the fleet traveled to the vicinity of the southern and northern Huangcheng Island and saw that the two islands were shrouded in a faint mist, and the peaks appeared one after another, beautiful and picturesque. Several cottages were exposed in the corrie, and plumes of smoke rose. Occasionally, a fisherman girl appeared on the mountain path, as if flying, what a beautiful fairyland.

太宗和侍从被这如诗如画的景色迷住，随行的玉玺太监，只顾观赏美景，被人挤碰，不慎失手，把捧在手中玉印掉进海里。太宗大吃一惊，急令军士打捞，怎奈隍城岛周围水深流急，半天也没打捞上来。只急得太宗心如油煎，当众道："孤家东征决不半路收兵，谁若捞得国宝，孤家重重有赏！"话音刚落，忽见海中"哗啦""哗啦"冒出串串水珠，泛起阵阵水花，大家正在惊奇，只见一条大鱼慢慢地浮出水面，头顶着大印游近龙船。军师拿过鱼头上的大印，太宗一看，果真是刚才掉进海里的玉玺，便立即命令全体将士，一起恭立船头，向那大鱼千呼万唤，感谢捞印之功。再看那大鱼头顶上，仍有清楚印痕，太宗赞道："好个知吾心，通朕意的鱼儿，今日献印有功，朕赐玉名'印鱼'，封'巡海将军'，可四海巡查，到各处龙宫领取俸禄！"天子代天行命，金口玉言，从此，印鱼（因它极像鲅鱼，又称"印鲅"）四海游巡，查处那些肆虐的海妖水怪，不法的虾兵蟹将，十分劳碌辛苦。幸好头顶的印痕乃天子玉玺的戳记，当有特殊功能，只要将这吸盘似的印痕吸在游鱼身下，行驶的船底，便可驾鱼乘船，畅游千里而不费吹灰之力。印鱼的不寻常的印记和特殊功能，传之子孙后代二百多年，享尽富贵荣华。唐朝衰亡以后，"巡海将军"一职也自行卸去，流传下来，只留下了"印鱼"的赐名和免费畅游的待遇了。

Taizong and his attendants were fascinated by the picturesque scenery. The jade seal eunuch accompanied only watched the beautiful scenery. and squeezed by others, causing the jade seal dropped from their hands into the sea. Taizong was astonished and hurriedly ordered the sergeant for salvage, but the water around Huangcheng Island was deep and rushing, and it can not be salvaged after long time of efforts. Taizong was so anxious that his heart was like being fried, and said in public: "I will not retreat halfway. If anyone who can salvage the national treasure, the lone family will be give a lot of rewards!" As soon as the voice fell, I suddenly saw "wow" and "wala" in the sea. Strings of water droplets came out, and there were waves of spray. Everyone was surprised, only to see a big fish slowly surfaced, swimming near the dragon boat with a big seal on its head. The military commander took the big seal from the fish's head. Taizong saw that it was indeed the jade seal that had fallen into the sea just now. He immediately ordered all the soldiers to stand up on the bow of the boat together, calling out to the big fish, thank it for the contribution in salvage of the seal. Looking at the big fish's head, there are still clear marks. Taizong praised: "A good fish who knows my heart and communicates with my will. Today, It present the seal with merit. I will give the jade name 'Seal fish' and called the 'Patrol General'. It can patrol all over the world, and go to various dragon palaces to receive salaries!" The emperor acted on behalf of the sky, and had valuable words, and from then on, Seal fish (because it is very similar to the Spanish mackerel, also known as "Seal Mackerel"). Traveling around the world, investigating the raging sea monsters and water monsters, illegal shrimp soldiers and crabs, it was a very hard work. Fortunately, the imprint on the top of the head was the stamp of the imperial jade seal. When any special function is required, just sucking the sucker-like imprint under the swimming fish, the bottom of the traveling boat can travel thousands of miles by the fish without any effort. The unusual mark and special functions of seal fish had been passed down to the descendants for more than two hundred years, enjoying riches and glory. After the decline and fall of the Tang Dynasty, the post of "Patrol General" was also removed, leaving only the name given to "Seal Fish" and the treatment of free swimming.

思考与实践

Thinking and practice

复述故事主要内容。

Retell the main content of the story.

利用假期寻找上述传说中的遗址。

Use the holiday to find the aforementioned legendary ruins.

第四课 张羽煮海
Lesson 4　Zhang Yu cooks the sea

很久很久以前,在庙岛群岛上,传颂着一个美丽的爱情故事。讲的是,古时候,广东潮州有一位书生,姓张名羽,表字伯腾。祖上曾是官宦殷实之家。早年父母双亡,有些家资田亩。自幼苦读寒窗,饱学诗文。长成却厌烦繁文缛节,嫌弃儒教八股,因而屡试不中。年近二十,孑然一身,只落得个落魄秀才。他索性离经叛道,四海游学。遍访高山大川,广游名胜古迹。因慕名渤海有仙山,来寻海市仙境。登上渤海诸岛,拜过沙门圣庙,尽览仙山神岛的山水风光。一日,带书童闲游海上,忽见一座古寺,临海耸立,群楼重阁,飞檐镏金,但见居中正门额上有"古佛寺"三个大字,赫然醒目。张生走近,向一小僧打揖道:"吾本东海落第秀才,闲游仙山神岛。请小师父报于长老,说小生特来相访。"张生拜过石佛寺法云长老之后,恳请道:"小生潮州人氏,自幼父母双亡,功名未遂,慕名来游仙岛。因见古寺清幽境界,乞望长老借一净室,与小生温习经文,不知尊意如何?"长老见秀才气宇轩昂,谈吐文雅,心中窃喜。忙应道:"寺中房舍尽有,让小僧去收拾东南幽静一处,正好与秀才观书习文也。"

A long time ago, there was a beautiful love story on the Miaodao Islands. It is said that in ancient times, there was a scholar in Chaozhou, Guangdong, whose name is Zhang Yu, with a style name of Boteng. The ancestors used to be the home of officials and officials. Both parents died in the early years, leaving some wealth and lands. Since childhood, he studied hard and was well versed in poetry and prose. When he grew up, he was tired of red tape and disliked the stereotypes of Confucianism, so he failed repeatedly. Nearly twenty years old, lonely, only a downright talented person. He simply deviated from the Scriptures and traveled all over the world. Visiting the mountains and rivers, and traveling to places of interest. Because he always admires the fairy mountains in the Bohai sea, he came to find the wonderland of the sea city. Climbing to the Bohai Islands, visiting the temple of Shamen, and enjoying the scenery of Xianshan Island. One day, he took a child with a book to travel on the sea, and suddenly saw an ancient temple, erected aside the sea, a group of buildings and pavilions, and gilded eaves, but saw the three large characters "Ancient Buddhist Temple" on the forehead of the central main entrance, which was strikingly eye-catching. Zhang Sheng approached and said to a young monk: "I am a talented person in the East China Sea and take a leisurely tour of the fairy mountain and the island. Please report to the elders and say that I am here to visit." Zhang Sheng paid homage to the elder Fayun of Shifo Temple. Pleaded: "I'm Chaozhou people, both parents died since childhood, failed to achieve fame, and came to visit Immoral island admiringly. Seeing the quiet state of the ancient temple, begging the elders to borrow a clean room to study the scriptures for me, I don't know you will afree?" The elders were delighted when they saw the talent and his elegant talk. He responded quickly: "There are many empty houses in the temple. Let the little monk go to clean up a quiet place in the southeast, just to read and study for you."

张生住进寺内，倍觉僧家愫雅，俱无闲人嘈杂，且宽敞洁净，十分满意。用过斋饭，遂叫书童，取得琴来，净手焚香，灯下抚音一曲，消遣散心。

Zhang Sheng lived in the monastery, and felt that the monk's home was elegant, free from noisy people, spacious and quiet, and very satisfied. After eating vegetarian food, he called his book boy, got a yre, cleaned his hands, burned incense, and played a song under the lamp to relax.

事有凑巧，东海水宫的龙王三公主，恰在这秋风习习，月朗星稀的夜晚，却心有浮躁，不思寝睡，带着侍女，飘离龙宫。轻移莲步，脚踩矶珠，漫游仙山海边，观赏着明月下的神岛夜景。忽闻清奇幽雅、悲壮悠长的琴声在夜空中漂飞。主仆来到佛寺窗前，但见敞开的窗扉里，灯下一位飘逸俊美少年，正端坐专心抚琴敲韵，如醉如痴，若入仙境。室内弹得出神入化，窗外听得迷情流连，曲犹未终，只闻"刮喇"一声响，琴弦断绝了一根。张生大惊："敢是有人窃听？"出门见那女子，十分惊讶，脱口而出："好一位仙女下凡也！"忙整襟正冠作揖："请问小娘子,谁氏之家,如何夜行到此?"龙女羞怩作答:"委身龙氏三姑娘,小字琼莲,闻见公子弹琴,迷恋佳音妙韵,不想惊扰,还望恕罪。""不妨事。小娘子既为听琴而来,这等是赏琴知音的了,何不屈尊书房中小坐,待小生细弹一曲,乞望赐教。"龙女进房坐定,笑问张生:"敢问先生高姓?"张生诚恳答道:"小生姓张名羽,字伯腾,潮州人氏。自幼苦读诗书,求取功名未遂,游学至此。父母双亡,尚无妻室。若小娘子不嫌弃小生落第贫寒,赐嫁与我为妻,可否?"龙女沉吟多时,低头垂眉作答:"我见公子聪明智慧,英伟俊雅,甘愿与你为妻。实则父母在堂,等我禀问二老,征得他们应允。到八月十五日中秋节,你来我家,招你为婿,了却你我的终生意愿。"张生喜不自禁:"承蒙小娘子俯允,小生万分感激,只望言而有信。俺张生可是个志诚老实之人呀!"龙女也云:"妾也非水性杨花、朝三暮四之辈。既许你为妻,决不失信。妾有冰蚕织就的鲛蛸帕送你,权为信物。望君中秋佳节,在这海边屈候。届时将有迎亲水族,接你去龙宫拜见父母做成你我的终身大事。切记,切记!万万不中失约。"才子佳人,信誓旦旦,上待佳日良宵,成就百年之好。

By coincidence, the third princess of the Dragon King lived in Donghai Water Palace, just in this autumn breeze, moonlight and starry night, was a little slighty and impetuous, did not want to sleep, took the maid, and floated away from the dragon palace. Moving her lotus step lightly, stepping on the rocky beads, roaming on fairy mountains and seaside, and watching the night view of the god island under the bright moon. Suddenly, the peculiar, elegant, tragic and long-lasting sound of lyre was flying in the night sky. They came to the window of the Buddhist temple, saw through the open window, an elegant and handsome young man under the lamp, sitting upright and concentrating on playing the lyre he was fascinated, as if staying in a fairyland. Playing indoors is superb and, listening outside the window was lingering, the song was still not ended, only a "scratch" sound, the string was cut off. Zhang Sheng was shocked: "someone eavesdropped?" When he went out to see the woman, he was very surprised, and blurted out: "What a fairy going to the world!" The Dragon Girl replied shyly: "I was the third girl of the Dragon king, named Qionglian, just heard the lyre playing, and very infatuated with the good music and rhyme; and I don't want to interrupt, and hope your forgiveness. " " I don't mind and I will, why not come to my study room, and I will play a song for you, and beg for your advice. " The dragon girl entered the room and sat down and asked Zhang Sheng with a smile: "What's your name?" Zhang Sheng replied sincerely: "I'm Zhang Yu, with a style name of coming here for visit. Boten, and is a Chaozhou native. Since childhood, he has been studying poetry and fame and has failed to obtain fame, coming here for visit. Both parents have died and there is no wife. If you do not dislike my poorness, marry me as my wife, can you?" The Dragon Girl pondered for a long time, bowed her eyebrows and replied: "I see your wisdom and wisdom, heroic and handsome appearance, and are willing to be a your wife. In fact, I must get their permission from my parents. By the Mid-Autumn Festival on August 15th, you come to my house to recruit you as son-in-law, realizing our life-long wishes." Zhang Sheng couldn't help but be overjoyed: "Thank you for your permission, I am extremely grateful, and only hopes to believe in words. I am a sincere and honest person!" The dragon girl also said: "I'm sune to keep my words. I send you a silk worm handker chief as a token. I wish you to be then at this seaside. At that time, there will be a welcoming family who will take you to the Dragon Palace to meet my parents and make you and me a lifelong event. Remember! Never miss an appointment. "Gifts and beautiful ladies, vowed to wait the good day. "

时隔数日,兵分两头。正是张生焦急等待,度日如年。此时刻,龙宫那边却是风云变幻,是非如愿。那龙王爱这小女如掌上明珠,怎能应允下嫁于落魄的凡人书生。龙女先是如实禀报参秀才的人品才学,跪求父王应允。继而,决然正色声明非张生不嫁,以死抗争。龙王再三劝说未成,雷霆大发,下令把这不孝无规的娇女关锁深宫闺房,派兵把守,不准龙女越雷池一步。此刻龙王的怒气未消,怨恨不了乃要封海锁岛,使张生、龙女不得相见,让他等死了这门心思。他出得龙宫,向大海吼叫数声,刹那间,天海骤变,波涛汹涌,海浪翻滚,直搅得天昏地暗,日月无光。海岛岸边站不得人,行不得路。

A few days have passed. Zhang Sheng was waiting anxiously, passing the day like a year. At this moment, the situation on the Dragon Palace was changing, and things were not as expected. The dragon king loved this little girl like a jewel in his palm, how can he agree to marry a fallen mortal scholar. The dragon girl first reported truthfully regarding the talents of the scholars, and begged her father for permission. Then, she resolutely declared that if not permitted she would fight desperately. When the dragon king tried to persuade her and failed, furiously ordered the unfilial and unruly girl to be locked in the deep palace and sent soldiers to guard it, and the dragon girl was not allowed to cross the thunder pond. At this moment, the dragon king's anger had not disappeared, and the resentment can't be suppressed, he wanted to seal the sea and locked the island, so that Zhang Sheng and the dragon girl can't see each other, and let him wait until death. He got out of the Dragon Palace and roared to the sea several times. In an instant, the sky and the sea changed suddenly, the waves were turbulent, and the waves rolled, making the sky dark and dark, and the sun and the moon were dark. There were no people standing on the shore of the island, no way to go.

眼看佳期已到,海上还是风去浪高,龙女向天音信传来。张生心急如焚、坐卧不宁。他跪在盘陀石下,面向大海,声泪俱下,苦苦哀求,并不见大风有所减弱,巨浪悄然静停。更望石等意中人的踪影。他抱着盘陀石心焦肠断、冥思苦等,一连几天不吃不喝,不胜不息,嗓子喊哑了,眼泪哭干了,几次昏厥过去。方丈书童反复劝说开导,再三搀扶拖拉,张生死活不肯回房歇息,豁上一死,也要等来龙女消息。

Seeing that the best time was here, the wind was still going up and the waves were high on the sea. Zhang Sheng was anxious and restless. He knelt under the Pantuo stone, facing the sea, crying and pleading, but the strong wind did not weaken, and the huge waves stopped a little. He was waiting for the trace of the person he likes. He held the stone, heartbroken, contemplated, and waited for a few days without eating or drinking, endlessly, his voice became dumb, his tears were dry, and he fainted several times. The abbot repeatedly persuaded and enlightened, and dragged, Zhang Sheng refused to go back to the room to rest, and still waited for the dragon girl news.

这事被镇守渤海海峡四个海域通道的龟鳖鼋鼍四兄弟得知。三兄长知这风浪有些来头,都聪明知趣地躲开了。唯独这憨厚老实的鼍老弟,听了张生的叙说，顿起恻隐之心，暗自思忖："这样的郎才女貌，这般忘我痴情，吾理当全力相助，玉成良缘。"它让张生骑上鼋背，劈开风浪，径直来到龙宫殿外，可龙门紧锁。张生进不去，龙女也出不来，无奈之下，张生拿出鲛蛸帕，几经晃动，震动了龙宫。探子报来，那龙王只气得两眼冒火，咬牙切齿地骂道："好个鼋龟孙子，不知好歹的东西！平日里见你忠厚老实，委你重任，你怎么这样吃里爬外，坏我龙宫大事。撤掉你珍珠门海域镇守一职，往北发配一百里，永远锁锢在渤海之中。"龙王重罚鼋龙，恶气仍未消减，怒喷一口，将张生抛向海空，重重地摔回到沙门岛岸边，昏死过去。

This matter was learned by the four brothers who guarded the four sea areas of the Bohai Strait. The three elder brothers knew that the storm had something to do, and they all avoided wisely. Only this honest brother, listened to Zhang Sheng's narration, felt compassionate, and thought: "This kind of man and woman, so selfless and infatuated, I should help each other with all my strength, and become a good match." It made Zhang Sheng ride on. by splitting the wind and waves, he went straight to the outside of the Dragon Palace, but the dragon door was locked tightly. Zhang Sheng couldn't get in, and the Dragon Girl couldn't get out. In desperation, Zhang Sheng took out the shark papyrus, shaking it several times. When the spies reported, the dragon king only got angry with his eyes and gritted his teeth and cursed: "What a ghost grandson, you don't know what is good or bad! I see you are loyal and honest on weekdays, and entrust you with a heavy responsibility. Why are you eating like this and ruining my Dragon Palace? Removing your role of guarding of the Pearl Gate sea area, sending to a hundred miles north, and be locked in the Bohai Sea forever." The Dragon King punished it heavily, but the evil spirit had not diminished. Back to the shore of Shamen Island, and become unconscious.

不知几个时辰，张生朦胧地觉得仿佛有玉手在轻轻拂胸，樱口在缓缓输气，他慢慢地从昏迷中苏醒过来，但见仙女正在抢救自己醒来。他忘情地呼喊："琼莲来也！琼莲救我！"那女子说道："贫道既非龙女，亦非凡人，吾乃秦时宫人。当年，曾为始皇采炼长生不老之药，来这仙山神岛。恨那秦王暴政害民，遂埋名隐居，不再返回。百年不食人间烟火，修成大道。毛发皆白，体态轻捷，腾云驾雾，来去自如。身带法物,济世行善。仙界世人,皆称我"毛女仙姑"。今奉东华上仙法旨,要我来指引你还归正道。"张生谢过,道:"小生凡胎肉眼,不识上仙指引,乞望恕罪。"仙姑道:"我且问你,那听琴女子乃东海龙王最宠爱的小女,岂肯与你有夫妻缘分?"张生回答:"既没缘分,她怎肯约我八月十五夜,到她家,招我为婿,又与我这鲛绡帕做信物?像她这样端庄文雅的龙宫娇女,岂能滥情允婚与我?"仙姑道:"这鲛绡手帕,果是龙宫之物。想来那龙女看你中意了。只是这龙王恶性暴躁,怎能容易地把爱女嫁你为妻,龙女不来接你,也无音信传来,定是被贬罚锁禁起来,使你们不得相见。罢,罢,罢!我帮人帮到底,行善行到家。送你三件法物:银锅一只,金钱一文,铁勺一把。你选一临海洁净之处,将锅支将起来,用铁勺将海水舀进锅里,放金钱在锅水中,加火烧之。锅水热则大海热,水沸则海也沸。锅内水,若煮去一分,大海水则落下十丈,煮去二分,落下二十丈,若煮干了锅底,则大海便要见底了。那龙王怎么还能坐得住呢?必然令人来请,招你为婿也。"

After long time, Zhang Sheng dimly felt as if a jade hand was gently brushing his chest, making artificial respiration for him; and he slowly recovered from the coma, but saw that the fairy was rescuing himself and woke up. He exclaimed with emotion, "Qionglian come! Qionglian save me!" The woman said: "I was neither a dragon girl, but also an extraordinary person. I am a member of the Palace during Qin dynasty. Back then, I used to work for the first emperor to live forever. The medicine, come to this fairy mountain island. I hate that king Qin's tyranny that harms the people, so I live in seclusion and never return. I have been other worldy for a hundred years. The hair is white, by the body is light, the clouds and the fog, come and go freely. Things, help the world and do good. People in the world of immortality call me 'Female celestial'. Today, I am ordered by Donghua celestial to guide you to return to the right way." Zhang Sheng thanked him and said: "Xiaosheng is born with naked eyes, but I don't know. The gods will guide you and beg for forgiveness." she said: "I ask you, the girl is the girl who is most beloved by the Dragon King of the East China Sea, how will she have a relationship with you as a husband and wife?" Zhang Sheng replied, "If there is no fate, how could she agree to ask me to come to her house on the 15th night of

August, recruit me as son-in-law, and give the token to me? How can a dignified and elegant dragon palace girl like her marry me indiscriminately?" She said: "This handkerchief is realy from the dragon palace. I see the dragen girl will certainly like you. It's just that the dragon king is vicious and violent. How can you easily marry his love daughter as your wife? If the dragon girl doesn't come to pick you up, and there is no news came, she must have been degraded and locked up, preventing you from seeing each other. You may rest assured! I will help you to the end. I will give you three magic weapons: a silver pot and a penny of money and an iron spoon. You choose a clean place near the sea, hold the pot up, scoop the sea water into the pot with an iron spoon, put the money in the pot water, add fire to it. The hot pot water makes the sea hot, and the boiling water makes the sea also boiling. If the water in the pot drops 10% by boiling, the sea water will drop ten zhang, and if the bottom of the pot is exposed, the sea will be also like this. How can the dragon king sit down? Where to live? It is bound to invite you to be your son-in-law."

　　张生接来法物，再三谢过上仙的神助指教。精神为之一振，浑身也轻松来劲了。他叫来书童，在庙岛南端面东临海的盘陀石旁，用三角石驾起锅子，用铁勺舀那海水，填满了银锅，再放入金钱；书童用火镰引燃火种，柴木便着起火来。书童猛然想起，那夜龙女临别，侍女偷送予他一把蒲扇，他也权作信物。如今正好用来煽风助火之用。果然，只轻摇数下，那火便十分旺盛，锅里的水，便迅速地热将起来。说来称奇，这边烧锅煮水，那边大海也随之变热。不一会儿，书童喜叫："锅里水沸了也！"张生试看那海里动静，果然海水也翻腾沸滚。正应着仙姑所言。张生且喜又忧，喜的是，滚热的海水，龙王按耐不住，必求饶允亲。忧的是，那龙女也在宫中，她娇身纤弱，怎能耐得了这般沸热。正在犹豫之际，忽见石佛寺长老气喘吁吁，急奔而来，边跑边叫："秀才，手下留情！快快撤柴熄火。天大的事情，都可以好好商量！"长老近得前来，"阿弥陀佛！秀才呀，你听我说，方才，东海龙王，遣人告急。说一秀才，不知用什么物件，煮得海水滚沸，热得那龙王无处逃躲，央求老僧，劝住秀才，休要再煮海了，你想要干什么，龙王尽可应允。"张生道："师傅长老，我老实对你说，我本来也不愿烧锅煮海，惊扰水国生灵，那琼莲也无可幸免。只是，那龙王若不应允我等的亲事，我便只管加火烧锅，直煮见那海底方休。看你这龙王再凶恶狂躁到何时？"长老劝道："这事也不算为难。只要你停火烧锅，跟我去水国龙宫，我愿作红媒，定能成就这桩美满良缘。"

Zhang Sheng received them, and thanked the gods for her help. The spirit was refreshed, and the whole body was relaxed. He called the book boy, and he used a triangle stone to support the pot, with a triangular stone next to the Pantuo stone on the south end of the temple island, and used an iron spoon to scoop up the sea water and fill it to fill the silver pot in which the money is added then. The book boy ignited the fire with a steel for flint, The book boy suddenly remembered that the dragon girl parted and the maid gave him a cattail leaf fan, and also as a token. Now it was just used to fan the fire. Sure enough, just shaking it a few times, the fire was very strong, and the water in the pot quickly heated up. It was amazing to say that when you boiled water in a pot here, the sea on the other side will also become hot. After a while, the book boy happily cried: "The water in the pot is boiling!" Zhang Sheng tried to see the movement in the sea, and the sea was also boiling. Just as the celestial said. Zhang Sheng was happy and worried. The happy thing was that the scorching sea water made the Dragon King unbearable and must beg for mercy. The worry was that the dragon girl was also in the palace, she was delicate, how can she endure such a boiling heat. While hesitating, he suddenly saw the elder of Shifo Temple panting and rushing forward, shouting as he ran: "Please, be merciful! Quickly remove the firewood and put out the fire, and anything can be discussed well." The elder came close."Amituofo! please, listen to me, just now, the Dragon King of the East China Sea, send people to tell me, the sea is boiling, and the dragon king has nowhere to escape. He begged me to persuade you don't cook the sea again. What do you want to do? The Dragon King can agree to it." Zhang Sheng said: "Master, I honestly tell you that I didn' t want to cook the sea and disturb the creatures of the water country. It' s also inevitable. However, if the Dragon King refuses to allow me to wait for the marriage, I will just add the hot pot and cook until the bottom of the sea is shown. See you when the Dragon King is ferocious and manic again?" The elder persuaded: "It's not difficult. As long as you stop cooking the pot and follow me to the Dragon Palace of the Water Country, I am willing to be a red matchmaker, and you will surely achieve this happy marriage."

仙岛岸边这般苦苦劝说，海里龙王听得真切明白。暗自思忖："这秀才也不同凡人，痴情苦恋，尚有神助；小女一见钟情，宁死相随；水国龙宫又处于危难之际，老王也只好顺水推舟，答应这桩亲事罢了！"急急下令，快快调集一干迎亲人马，去那海上仙山，接那新姑爷，荣登龙宫，拜堂成亲便了。

The Dragon King heard explicitly about the persuade on the shore of island. Secretly thinking: "This talent is also different from a mortal, infatuated with love, and still has a divine help; the little girl falls in love at first sight and would rather go with death; the dragon palace is in distress, the old king has no choice but to push the boat along the water and agree to this marriage!" Ordered, quickly mobilize a team for wedding, go to the fairy mountain, welcome the son-in-law, go to the Dragon Palace and hold the wedding ceremony.

到了这时，龙王也确有悔意。想那鼍龙"风浪送亲"，也确是好心行善，本王错怪误罚了它，着实惭愧！即刻遣人去渤海之中，请回它来，先参加喜宴，后事再议。那小鼍也是聪颖的精灵，心想"那龙王生性多疑猜忌，反复无常；三兄长各怀鬼胎，明哲保身，见死不救。请我回去贺喜，当能恢复功名，一生做个镇海守备，听人遣使，受人制约。自己的抱负难以施展，一生平庸无为。别个只当咱是无能无用之辈。如此这般，于事无补，无已何益？不如就此修炼造化成一方岛屿，造福岛上的黎民百姓。虽吃苦清贫，却能千古留名，何乐而不为也！"想到这里，它拒辞龙王之邀，立志据守渤海之中，慢慢炼化成为"海上仙山"的一个大岛。形似鼍龙伏卧海中，昂首向东，平背椭圆宽厚，一只短尾翘出海面，（人称小鼍子）。无论是从南面远看，还是在北边遥望，确是巨鼍出水无疑。所以，在唐朝以前，民间就叫作"鼍岛"。

At this time, the Dragon King indeed regret it. It was indeed good intentions of Tuo dragon "sending relatives by wind and waves". I punished it by mistake, and was really ashamed! Sending people to the Bohai immediately, inviting it to come back, attending the wedding banquet first, and discussing other things later. That little Tuo was also a smart elf, thinking "the dragon king is suspicious and capricious by nature, the three elder brothers are conceived, wise to protect themselves, and they will do nothing to save me from danger. Inviting me go back, when my fame will certeinly be restored, and be a defense of the sea would be all my life. I would listen to the orders from and are constrained by others. My ambitions are difficult to display, and my life is mediocre. It is better to cultivate and transform in an island, to benefit the people on the island. Despite hardships and poverty, My name will renain immortal, why not do it!" Thinking of this, it refused to resign from the Dragon King's invitation, determined to defend the Bohai and progressively refine it into a "sea fairy mountain". It looked like a dragon lying in the sea, with its head held high to the east, with a flat back elliptical and wide, and a short tail raised out of the sea. Whether it was viewed from a distance from the south or the north distantly, it was undoubtedly that the giant Tuo came out of the water. Therefore, before the Tang Dynasty, it was called "Tuodao" in folks.

千百年来，几经沧桑，"鼍变海岛"的故事失传，岛上人，嫌鼍与龟鳖同类，有伤大雅，那鼍字又生僻难书，故改作"砣矶岛"。细想起来，可真辜负了那鼍龙的一番善心美意了。

For thousands of years, after several vicissitudes of life, the story of "Tuo turns into an island" had been lost. The people on the island suspected that the meaing of Tuo was similar to the tortoise and turtle, which offends against good taste, and the word was uncommon and difficult to write, so it was changed to "Tuoji Island." When thought about it, The good expectation of Tuo drafon was really disappointed.

插话的工夫，海面风平浪静，碧蓝如镜，一支浩浩荡荡的迎接大队，披红褂绿，鼓乐齐鸣。千百水族皆打扮得焕然一新，喜气洋洋簇拥着一龙头宝驹，珠光宝气的彩鞍上，端坐着头戴花翎，身着红袍的张秀才。大红绸带扎结着红花彩球，斜挂前胸，好一副新郎官的气派。那水晶宫大殿内外，更是张灯结彩，鞭炮震天，鼓乐齐鸣。正堂之上，摆放着精工巧制的龙凤交首攀足，缠绕着大红喜字。侍女、伴娘搀出红装素裹的娇娘龙女。张生见到了数日坐禁绝食不得相逢的琼莲。二位悲喜交集，相拥而泣。良久，携手叩拜龙王、龙母。心中默默祷谢东华上仙、毛女仙姑、法云长老，更有那多情行善的鼍龙。

In the time of the interruption, the sea which was calm and blue was like a mirror, and a mighty greet brigade, dressed in red and green, came up, accompanied by the music of drum beats. Thousands of aquariums were all dressed up with a new look. They were beamingly surrounded by a dragon-headed treasure horse. On a jeweled saddle, the bridegroom sit there, wearing a flower feather on his head and a red robe. The red ribbon was tied with a red colored ball and hung on the front of the chest obliquely, giving it the style of a bridegroom. Inside and outside the main hall of the Crystal Palace, there were lights and festoons, firecrackers blasted to the sky and drums rang. On the main hall, there were exquisitely crafted dragons and phoenixes to climb the foot, entwined with the big red character of happiness. The maid and the bridesmaid accompanied the red-clad dragon girl. Zhang Sheng saw Qiong Lian who had been on a hunger strike for several days and could not meet each other. They met each other and cried. For a long time, They hand in hand to worship the Dragon King and Dragon Mother. In my heart, I prayed silently to Donghua celestial, The Hairy Girl Fairy, Fayun Elder, and even the kind-hearted Tuo dragon.

龙王面有愧色，急道：“罢了，罢了！你等素不相识，一见钟情，定是前世有缘。虽经磨难，至死不渝，足见信诚情笃。老王错待你们了。既成一家，不必计牵前嫌。以后日久天长，好心必有好报，有情人终成眷属啊！”

The dragon king looked ashamed and said anxiously: "You never knew each other, and fell in love at first sight, you must be destined in a previous life. Despite the hardships, you will remain faithful and sincere. I had treated you by mistake. We had become a family, don' t worry about it. In the days to come, good intentions will be rewarded, and lovers will eventually become family members!"

“恭喜！贺喜！”伴着哄钟般的话音，一位鹤发银须童颜的老者，疾步迈进大殿喜堂。龙王等众，见是东华上仙驾到，急忙上前揖迎。上仙微笑作答：“神龙，听俺吩咐。那琼莲非是你女儿，张生也非是你女婿，他等前世乃瑶池的金童玉女。则一念思凡，谪罚下界。如今偿还凤契，便着他等早离水府，重返瑶池；共证前因，同归仙位去也！”

"Congratulations! Congratulations!" Accompanied by a bell-like voice, an old man with a crane-haired silver beard and a childlike face hurried into the hall. When the dragon king and others saw that Donghua celestial arrives, they hurried forward to greet him. Donghua smiled and replied: "dragon king, listen to my instructions. Qionglian is not your daughter, and Zhang Sheng is not your son-in-law. In their previous life were the golden boy and jade girl of jade pool. They intend to enjoy worldly pleasures, and punished to the lower realm. Now It's time for them to go back and serve as immortals!"

张生、琼莲再拜龙王等族,追随东华上仙腾云驾雾西天去也!

Zhang Sheng and Qiong Lian worshipped to the Dragon King and other tribes, and followed Donghua's celestial and went to the west in the fog!

此神话故事称奇,这苦恋情缘叫绝。因而,千百年来流传。元朝文人李作古,据此编成元曲"沙门岛张生煮海"的杂剧。历朝各代,均有各种戏剧,争相编说,流传甚广。"沙门岛张生煮海,水晶宫龙女招婿",代代誉为爱情楷模,世世传为美谈佳话。

This myth was amazing, and this bitter love was amazing. Therefore, it had been circulated for thousands of years. Li Zuogu, a literatus in the Yuan dynasty, compiled a opera of the Yuan tune "Shamen Island Zhang Sheng cooks the sea". Throughout the dynasties, were various dramas, which were compiled coustantly, and they widely spread. "Shamen Island Zhang Sheng cooks the sea, Crystal Palace dragon daughter recruits son-in-law", he had been praised as a model of love for generations, and had been passed down from generation to generation.

🌊 思考与实践

Thinking and practice
复述故事主要内容。
Retell the main content of the story.
利用假期寻找上述传说中的遗址。
Use the holiday to find the aforementioned legendary ruins.

第六单元　科学·生活·实践

Unit 6　Science·Life·Practice

靠山吃山，靠海吃海；吃出海的科学，吃出海的文化。

Adhering the mountains and the sea, we eat rely on the mountains and the sea. The science and the culture of the sea are being.

第一课　怎样识别受污染的鱼
Lesson 1　How to Identify Contaminated Fish

含有化学物质的废水污染后,人一旦食用,就会发生急慢性中毒,甚至致死。鉴别鱼是否受到污染的方法是:

看鱼眼:未受到污染的鱼,鱼眼微突,富有光泽,黑白分明,受污染的鱼则眼球浑浊,失去原的光泽。严重污染的鱼,眼球明显外突。

看鳃:正常的鱼鳃鳃丝鲜红,排列整齐,而受到化学物质污染的鱼,鳃呈浅白色,其状粗糙。

看鱼尾:凡受到污染的鱼,其尾脊弯曲僵硬,成畸形

闻气味:正常鱼发出的是一种新鲜、湿润的腥味,而被污染的鱼散发出的是一种似氨味的气息或油味。

The fish pouuted by the wastewater containing chemical substances, once being eaten, will cause acute and chronic poisoning, even death. The method to identify whether the fish is contaminated is:

Look at the fish eyes: uncontaminated fish have slightly protruding, shiny, black-and-white eyes, while contaminated fish have muddy eyeballs and lose their original luster. Severely contaminated fish have their eyeballs extruded obvisusly.

Look at the gills: the gills of normal fish are bright red and neatly arranged, while the gills of the fish contaminated by chemicals are light white and rough in shape.

Look at the fish tail: any contaminated fish has a stiff tail ridge that is deformed

Smell the odor: Normal fish emits a kind of fresh. and moist fishy smell, while the contaminated fish emits an ammonia-like or an oily odor.

思考与实践

Thinking and practice

除了以上方法你还会用其他方法识别受污染的鱼吗？平时注意观察家中的鱼，学会鉴别鱼是否受到污染。

In addition to the above methods, do you still use other methods to identify contaminated fish? Pay attention to the fish in your home and learn to identify whether the fish is contaminated.

第二课 你会煎鱼吗
Lesson 2 Can You Fry Fish

　　煎鱼前,先将鱼用盐、酱油等调味液浸泡20分钟左右,煎时先把锅烧热,用生姜片把油锅擦一遍,再放食油;煎的过程中锅内要保持有油,不可干了锅,且始终保持"文火",向锅内不时淋点葡萄酒,可有效防止粘锅。

　　挂芡也是好办法。将鸡蛋打碎倒入盆中略加淀粉搅匀,再将鱼投入盆中,使鱼沾上一层蛋汁芡再煎,鱼皮也不会粘锅,煎出的鱼别具风味,色泽金黄,色香味俱全。

Before frying the fish, soaking the fish with salt and soy sauce and other seasonings for about 20 minutes firstly. When frying, firstly heating the pan, wiping the pan with ginger slices, and then adding the cooking oil, during the frying process, keeping the oil in the pan, do not make the pan burnt to dry, and always keep it on. "Slow fire", pouring some wine into the pot from time to time, which can effectively prevent the pot from sticking.

Hanging gorgon is also a good way. Breaking the eggs and pour them into a pot with a little starch and stirring well, then putting the fish in the pot, so that the fish is covered with a layer of egg sauce and then fried, the fish skin will not stick to the pan, the fried fish has a unique flavor and golden color and is golden yellow in color.

思考与实践

Thinking and practice
你吃过煎鱼吗?你会煎鱼吗?赶快做一盘煎鱼吧,让你的家人品尝品尝。

Have you ever eaten fried fish? Can you fry fish? Hurry up and make a plate of fried fish, let your family taste it.

第三课　哪些人不宜吃螃蟹
Lesson 3　Who Should Not Eat Crabs

螃蟹营养丰富,味道鲜美,但性寒,含有大量蛋白质和胆固醇,患有下列疾病者,以不吃或少吃蟹为宜:

① 伤风感冒、发烧、胃痛、腹泻者,如再食蟹会使病情加重。

② 慢性胃炎、十二指肠溃疡、胆结石、胆囊炎、肝炎活动期者,最好不吃或少吃,以免旧病复发或者转重。

③ 患有湿疹、皮炎、癣症、疮毒等皮肤病者,食蟹可能使病情恶化。

④ 对蟹过敏者应忌食。

⑤ 每百克蟹黄含有胆固醇高达 460 毫克,患有冠心病、高血压、动脉硬化、高血脂者,应不吃或少吃蟹黄。

⑥ 牙齿疼痛期间不宜吃蟹,尤其不能吃螯和腿,以防病情加重。

⑦ 生活不能自理、尤其是没牙的老人和孩子,不能由其自己食蟹,以防蟹皮哽喉。

⑧ 不可边食蟹边喝茶。因茶叶中含有鞣酸,与蟹肉中的蛋白质结合,会导致便秘,甚至致癌。

⑨有宿疾及冷积虚寒都忌食蟹。

Crabs are rich in nutrients and taste delicious, but they are cold in nature they contain a lot of protein and cholesterol, and the people suffering from the following diseases should avoid to eat or eat less crabs:

① People suffering from colds, fever, stomachache, diarrhea, if eating crabs, will make their condition worse.

② Those suffering from chronic gastritis, duodenal ulcer, gallstones, cholecystitis and active hepatitis should not eat or eat less, so as to avoid the recurrence of the old disease or making it more serious.

③ Those suffering from eczema, dermatitis, ringworm, and sores may make their state of illness even worse when eating crabs.

④ People who are allergic to crabs should not eat them.

⑤ Each 100 grams of crab roe contains cholesterol as high as 460 mg. Those suffering from coronary heart disease, high blood pressure, arteriosclerosis, and hyperlipidemia should not eat or eat less crab roe.

⑥ Crabs should not be eaten during tooth pain, especially pincers and legs, to prevent the condition from getting worse.

⑦ The elderly and children who cannot take care of themselves, especially the toothless elderly, cannot eat crabs on their own to prevent the crabs from choking their throats.

⑧ Do not drink tea while eating crabs. There are tannins in Chinese tea, which can combine with the protein in crab meat, causing constipation and even cancer.

⑨ If you have chronic diseases and cold accumulation, you should avoid eating crabs.

思考与实践

Thinking and practice

什么情况下不宜吃螃蟹。

你喜欢吃螃蟹吗？你是否在不宜吃螃蟹的情况下吃过它。

向你的长辈讲述吃螃蟹的小知识。

What circumstances should not eat crabs.

Do you like crabs? Have you ever eaten crabs when they are not suitable for you.

Tell your elders about eating crabs.

附录　诗文民谣

Appendix　Poems and Folk Songs

　　本附录记述了历代文人墨客对长岛的印记和海岛人民在生活生产中积累的民谣。学习了解这些诗歌民谣，就是熟悉海岛文化。

This appendix describes the imprints of literati and inkmen in the past dynasties on Changdao and the folk songs accumulated by the people of the island in life and production. To learn and understand these poems and folk songs is to learn the island culture.

第一课

北海十二石记

（宋）苏轼

登州下临大海。目力所及，沙门、砣矶、牵牛、大竹、小竹凡五岛，惟沙门最近，兀然焦枯，其余皆紫翠巉绝，出没涛中，真神仙所宅也。上生石芝、草木，皆奇玮，多不识名者。又多美石，五彩斑斓或作金色。熙宁己酉岁，李天章师中为登守。吴子野往从之游，时解二卿致政退居于登，使人入诸岛取石，得十二株，皆秀色粲然。适有舶在岸下，将转海至潮，子野请于解公，尽得十二石以归，置所居岁寒堂下。近世好事能致石者多矣，未有取北海而置南海者也。元祐八年八月十五日，东坡居士苏轼记。

漠岛记

（明）刘遵鲁

东镇区域最巨，泽润生民最薄，惟海而已。历代秩祭其来尚矣，故民间多立行祠。登州青之鱼盐地也，县治蓬莱。民濒海者奉海神尤切。海之半有山曰漠岛，庙曰灵祥，神曰显应神妃，耆民相传为东海广德王第七女。元得江南几二十载，粮运所过无风涛之险，岂非神明有以助之也。今太仓所蓄露积陈陈，富国裕民为古今冠，则吾神妃预有力焉。用勒坚珉以著厥美，当兴天地相为终始。

渔钓

（宋）慕维德

岛屿何清旷，
青青以竹名。
虾须簾可挂，
砣砚笔能耕。
煮茧开鬵味，
捞鱼鼓棹声。
春腥尝不厌，
动客忆莼情。

望仙门

（明）李愿

楼影空门里，
门开望众山。
绿鬟云漠漠，
翠黛月涓涓。
烟驾知何处，
星槎记昔年。
夕阳孤岛畔，
渺渺海浮天。

🌊 思考与实践

熟练背诵诗歌，谈谈每首诗所描写的景致。

第二课

观海市

（清）施闰章

蓬莱海市光有无，
仲冬物色夸大苏。
我亦再拜乞海若，
愿假灵迹看须臾。
是时苦旱海水渴，
神龙困懒枯珊瑚。
鼋鼓忽鸣津吏呼，
天吴出舞鲛人趋。
大竹盈盈横匹练，
小竹湛湛浮明珠。
方圆断续忽易位，
明灭低昂顷刻殊。
列屏复帐内宫阙，
桃源茅屋成村墟。
沙门小岛更奇绝，
浮屠倒影凌空虚。
有时离立为两人，
上者为笠下者车。
耄然双扉开白板，
中有琪树何扶疏。

三山十州一步地，
群仙冉冉来蓬壶。
神摇目眩看不定，
惜哉风伯为驱除。
人间快事亦如此，
浮云长据胡为乎？
　　噫嘻！
浮云长据胡为乎？

题砣矶砚

（清）乾隆

砣矶石刻五螭蟠，
受墨何须夸马肝。
设以诗中例小品，
谓同岛瘦与郊寒。

望海岭

（清）施闰章

苍茫登海嶠，
恍惚异人间。
岛屿浮天碧，
珊瑚照日般。
鲸波横作岸，
蜃气或成山。
的的群仙见，
蓬壶不可攀。

望海岭

（清）徐人凤

片帆缥缈漾层波，
隐隐三山点黛螺。
凫雁去边青霭远，
虬龙蜇处白云多。
数盘列峙渔矶稳，
一径悬崖鸟道过。
怅望尚余千古迹，
田横旧岛隐烟萝。

思考与实践

朗读这几首诗谈一谈你的感受。

第三课

题长岛
董必武

游竞长山岛，
心胸甚豁然。
天津寄锁钥，
旅顺结连环。
海角苍波远，
滩头白石圆。
军民和协好，
建县纪新编。

访长岛
贺敬之

长岛览秀如醋饮，
复我诗人少年心。
踏歌海市蜃楼境，
握手灵异神仙群。
一宿条条玉石街，
双睫层层珍珠门。
五载创业惊大步，
十年飞鸟信凌云。
朝见海田展画卷，
夜听涛声数足音。
此景此情不须酒，
长岛醉我动歌吟。

月牙湾
叶剑英

内长山岛月牙湾，
勤事渔农并石田。
昂价石球生异彩，
妇孺岂惜指头艰。

题月牙湾

赵朴初

水天一色月牙湾，
养殖精勤海作田。
不负穷研兼苦战，
天堂旗帜夺江南。

月牙湾

启功

一湾新月印滩涂，
水碧山青举世无。
仙境不须求物外，
行人步步踏明珠。

思考与实践

朗读这几首诗谈一谈你的感受。

收集歌颂长岛的歌词。

第四课 谚语

气像谚语

春打六九头,卖被去置牛。

春打五九尾,冻死鬼。

春冷秋热,必是雨工。

朝红不出门,夜红行千里。

夏至鱼齐,白露鸟齐。

东风夜向南(指风向转换)。

九里南风冻死鬼。

朝刮三(天),夜刮七(天),不晌不夜刮一日。

早上雾露头,晌午晒死牛。

不怕初一阴,就怕初二下。

九里雾露百日风(数九中如有雾日,一百天左右必有大风)

清明断雪不断雪,谷雨断霜不断霜。

紫微星(北极星)下打闪,刮风下雨不远。

大旱之年,忘不了五月十三(此日俗称是关老爷磨刀日,多下雨)

三月三,九月九,艄公不打江边走(指农历三月初三和九月初九左右必有大风)。

大雁不过三月三,小燕不过九月九(指大雁北去小燕南归的时间)。

东虹雾露,西虹雨,南虹来了发河水,北虹来了,割萝卜。

打了春别欢喜,还有四十天冷天气。

二月二,土地爷擒大褂(指农历二月初二左右必有大风)

三月三,清明暴(指农历三月初三左右必有大风)。

八月十五云遮月,正月十五雪打灯。

八月刁险九月稳,十月有个小阳春（农历八月风暴多,九月风暴相对减少,十月必有一段晴暖时间）。

处暑鹏子白露鹰,（指鹏鹰南过经海岛的时间）。

麦子上场,辣肉（指荔枝螺）上床（群聚成堆）。

天戏戏到顶,下雨下满井。

春风头秋风尾（春风来势凶猛,秋风后劲大）。

西风落日住,不住刮倒树。

潮汐谚语

十二三,正晌干,满了潮,黑了天。

十五六,吃晌儿以后（指干潮时间）

十八九,两头不得手（不宜赶海）。

二十四五黄昏满,吃了,早晌把靠赶。

月亮晌,潮不涨（指夜晚月亮如升入正空,海潮为最低潮）。

春发白航业发黑（春天白天西流大,秋季夜里西流大）。

初三水、十八潮,二十四五胡吊着（指农历初三和十作海水流大,二十四五海水流小）。

初一、十五,两头没有（指没有潮流）。

海猫子（海鸥）叫,潮水到。

歇后语

廷巴鱼好吃——牙硬。

海水冲了龙王庙——自家人不认自家人。

海猫子吃小鲫鱼——心满意足。

老王婆摸蟹子——望不着那一夹。

六月的牙偏鱼——臭美。

海蜇过河——随大流。

天津的小改撬——靠帮了。

网兜装鱼——探头坚脑。

小鱼穿大串——勒掉嘎齿（腮）。

提头、大冲（船帆上的副件）——各有各的用场

大筋作揽子（船尾部的副件）——大材小用

鱼中挑刺——没完没了

小猫吃小鱼——有头有尾

大主作猴头（帆船上拴缆的小木桩）——亏材料了。

八蛸吃蟹子——鼓盖了。

偷嘴的猫——不吃鱼也有腥味。

海里捞月亮——望空捕影。

船老大坐后艄——看风使船

船上的桅杆——直通通的。

思考与实践

朗读并背诵你喜欢的谚语、歇后语。